FEAST OF FIRE

THE FATHER'S DAY OUTPOURING

by

JOHN KILPATRICK

CONTENTS

Acknowledgments v

Foreword by Dr. David Yonggi Cho vii

Introduction ix

SECTION ONE: THE SPARK OF LIFE
Job 41:19

Chapter 1   A Father's Words in Georgia 3

Chapter 2   Hearing the Call 11

Chapter 3   A Godly Influence 19

SECTION TWO: FANNING THE FLAME
Isaiah 29:6

Chapter 4   Learning to Minister 33

Chapter 5   Building a House of Prayer 41

Chapter 6   Priestly Blessing 51

SECTION THREE: A FEAST OF FIRE
Acts 2:2-3

Chapter 7   Revival Falls 69

Chapter 8   Step Out of the Way 87

SECTION FOUR: THE FIRE SPREADS
Jeremiah 20:9 • Psalm 39:3

Chapter 9   Let the River Flow 107

Chapter 10   Warning Signs on the River 111

Chapter 11   The Fire Is Burning—Now What? .. 119

Chapter 12   Conclusion—The Fire Spreads 125

ACKNOWLEDGMENTS

—Without my faithful and supportive Congregation, there would be no book. Their willingness to accept the Holy Spirit's invitation to *"the feast of fire"* makes this story possible.

—My Pastoral Staff, Board of Directors and Council of Deacons for their encouragement and loyal support in all my endeavors.

—About a quarter of the way through this project, I realized what an undertaking it was so I sought guidance. I found it in Jo Kadlecek. She is a gift from God. Her editing skills and oversight helped this story come together. She treated this, my first book, as though it were her own.

—Jean McPhee, a new member of our church, a product of the Brownsville outpouring, for her endless hours of research and attention to detail.

—Karen Hurston, reading her book "Growing the World's Largest Church" inspired me to seek her expertise on how to go about writing a book.

—My good friend of many years, Steve Hill. Without his obedience in following God's call to come to Brownsville Assembly of God, there would be no story. God used Steve as the spark that started the fire.

—My Sweetheart, my wife, my best friend, Brenda,

the most supportive wife a minister could have. I credit her with setting the table for the *"feast of fire"*. God used her to inspire me. Upon seeing the work God ignited in her caused an insatiable hunger in me for a move of God.

—At the foundation of all God has done in my life, I credit to R. C. Wetzel, the greatest man I've ever known — my mentor.

FOREWORD

America has always been close to my heart. Thousands of American soldiers fought in the Korean War, many giving their lives so my country could be free. That is why I pray daily for America. That is why I lead my congregation of 700,000 to pray for America in our twelve weekly worship services.

When I was ministering in Seattle, Washington, in 1991, I became deeply concerned about the spiritual decline in America. I began to pray even more earnestly for revival in these United States. As I prayed, I felt the Lord prompt me to get a map of America, and to point my finger on the map. I found myself pointing to the city of Pensacola in the Florida panhandle.

Then I sensed the Lord say, "I am going to send revival to the seaside city of Pensacola, and it will spread like a fire until all of America has been consumed by it."

That revival fire has now come to Pensacola's Brownsville Assembly of God church. This book gives a clear account of that revival, communicated by a man who best knows what has occurred and is happening: Pastor John Kilpatrick.

Read this book with prayerful anticipation, and let God's Holy Spirit minister to you. God wants His revival fire to spread to you, to your church and to your city. In God's economy, the best is yet to come.

—Dr. David Yonggi Cho

FEAST OF FIRE

Introduction:
Thirsty Souls

God has visited us. What an extraordinary experience for anyone to be in the presence of God's glory. It is life-changing to meet the God of the Universe face to face. It is a revival of splendid proportion; truly a *feast of fire!*

Let me begin this book at the onset by stating frankly and forthrightly that I am not the most qualified person to pastor a revival. Yes, I did go to Bible college. I studied church history and I read scores of books on the subject; so, I do know something about it. I've taught on revival, preached about it, talked through it and hoped for it all my life; still, that does not necessarily qualify me to be the type of spiritual leader one would expect to read about when studying revivals. I do not possess the faith of a Charles Finney, the tenacity of Azuza Street's Daddy Seymour or the intuition of a Jonathan Edwards. I can only pray for such graces as these; and I have been praying.

For several years I have prayed that God would pour out His Holy Spirit on the church. (What pastor does not pray for that?) I have been thirsty to see God work in new, refreshing ways.

Since 1982, when I accepted the responsibility as senior pastor of Brownsville Assembly of God in Pensacola, Florida, I have asked our people to pray with me, that together we might know and experience more fully the presence of God. For the past three years we have met on a weekly basis to specifically pray for revival. Initially, I admit I was a little skeptical as to whether our members would favor a weekly Sunday night, *prayer-only* service. Admittedly, I also felt guilty about not preaching twice a day on Sunday. When a friend told me that Pastor David Yonggi Cho of Korea's Yoido Full Gospel Church, the world's largest church, had envisioned that a revival would begin in America in a small southern town called Pensacola, Florida, I was amazed.

In all honesty, I seriously wondered if revival would happen; and I certainly never expected one of this magnitude to occur. In a matter of weeks some 97,000 men, women, boys, girls, teenagers, grandparents, friends, neighbors, co-workers and family members have visited our evening worship services for the first time. Thus far we have recorded more than 10,000 conversions to Jesus Christ. I have been astounded to see that in spite of my suspicions and skepticism God has had mercy on me and I know, like the thousands of others who have been a part of this great *feast of fire*, I will never be the same. Why? Because God has visited us.

Each night as I walk into the Brownsville Assembly of God Sanctuary on West DeSoto Street my emotions are overwhelmed and my mind is boggled as I witness the shoulders of our ordinarily *cool and macho* teenage boys shake uncontrollably under the supernatural power of Jesus. I observe wealthy businessmen in expensive suits as they kneel and weep. The Holy Spirit takes the words of forgiveness and grace spoken by our evangelist, Steve Hill, and imparts peace and reconciliation to those who are troubled and distressed. I watch elderly women and young mothers dance in the Lord, small children laugh and raise their hands in highest praise. Drug addicts and prostitutes fall to the floor prostrate before God, as they confess the hope of Christ for the first time in their lives.

Since our initial service on Father's Day, 1995, when revival began suddenly and spontaneously, and almost every night since (it is November, 1995, as I write this), thousands of people have come from all over the country and around the world. Dozens of denominations have been represented as we have seen people from all walks of life and from diverse ethnic and economic backgrounds come to *the fountain*, to get a taste of God's presence in these remarkable and extraordinary services. It is a wonder to behold. It is revival, a *feast of fire!*

As I look out over the audience each night, I am deeply touched as I see both familiar and unfamiliar faces worshipping God with incredible freedom, yearning for more of Jesus and willing to allow His Spirit to move in their lives. In ways that might seem foolish or strange to an outsider, these friends of all ages are experiencing an unprecedented outpouring of God's Holy Spirit in their lives. With arms extended toward heaven, tears streaming down their faces, their voices singing and their hearts fixed upon the Master, they drink of the *living water*. Thirsty souls are satisfied. God is manifesting Himself in ways I could never have imagined. How did it come about? One thing is for certain; it did not happen overnight.

No revival in history has ever *just happened!* **Prayer always precedes a great move of God.** The Holy Spirit heralds the call, the people of God heed the call and then God Almighty responds to the call, and this is what we have seen at Brownsville Assembly of God.

As I mentioned earlier, I feel like the most unlikely person in the world to pastor a revival; but in retrospect I believe there are several events in my own life and in the life of our church that have precipitated these marvelous revival meetings. God's Spirit has long been at work, preparing the way for all of us to be a part of this extraordinary spiritual milestone. Consequently, I am humbled and graciously privileged to see the Lord's presence and glory so powerfully manifested during our Pensacola services.

It is my hope and prayer that this book will provide the context for understanding such a mighty move of God during these challenging and exciting times.

As a small boy, I had no idea what God had in store for me if I would simply love Him. I knew my soul was thirsty. Perhaps here is where the story of the Pensacola Revival begins.

Section One

The Spark of Life

*"Out of his mouth go burning lamps,
and **sparks of fire** leap out."* Job 41:19

Chapter One

A Father's Words in Georgia

I was only eight years old the first time my daddy left our family. I will never forget standing on the street outside our small Columbus, Georgia, home and hearing him shout at my mother. A tear trickled down my face as I heard him scream ugly names at her. She stood just under five feet tall, somewhat slight and frail, but a tenacious woman of Native American descent. I sat down on the curb outside our little three bedroom house at 1603 50th Street, and wished for the yelling to stop. I was afraid for my mamma.

For some reason, my daddy could be especially mean in moments like these; other times, he was a good man, a hard working father who tried to do right by his family; but when Mamma started taking us to the Eighth Street Assembly of God Church to teach us about Jesus, Daddy did not like it and decided to stay away. Now we were about to be alone.

"Lord," I cried. I remembered the Sunday School lessons about praying when my heart hurt, "I won't have a daddy anymore." I blinked back another tear, bit my lip and sat paralyzed on the cement sidewalk in our low-income neighborhood. It was a hot Georgia afternoon when my father first left us; it was hotter still inside me. I didn't know what to do.

Suddenly, I felt a comforting warmth on my shoulder, like a huge hand patting down my fears, and offering me a cold cup of water. Somehow, I knew God was answering my prayer. "Don't be afraid," He whispered to my young heart. "I'll take you up and I'll be your Father."

At that instant, Mamma walked out of the house with all the dignity she could muster. She took my hand. "Son, things are going to be okay," she said. "God is still with us." I looked into her pretty face, her smooth dark skin radiating in spite of her pain, "Okay, Mamma," I whispered. I knew with eight year-old confidence that she was right.

Growing Pains

Shortly after that first separation, my mother took us children to my grandparents' home out in the country. They lived in Alabama. My older half-sisters and I stayed there while my mamma stayed in the city and worked to get her life back together. It was particularly difficult for me because my grandparents seemed old and they didn't have any neighbors close by, let alone any young children for me to play with. In my old neighborhood I loved playing ball and fishing in the nearby stream with the other kids but here I was left pretty much to myself. At my grandparent's place, it was lonely and quiet. I was not sure when I would ever see my mamma again, or my daddy for that matter.

Three months later, however, Mamma came

back for us. Daddy also came back too, at least on and off, but for the next four years my parents struggled and fought. Daddy would leave and come back until, eventually, he left for good. Finally, they were divorced.

By the time I was twelve years old, Mamma had gotten a full time job scrubbing floors at the Restmere Nursing Home. She earned only minimum wage, "But it was work," she said. With little more than a sixth grade education, job possibilities were limited. She had been forty years old when she gave birth to me, so now life as a fifty-two year-old single mother was giving Mamma quite a challenge.

Still, Mamma received enough joy in taking us to worship services at the Eighth Street Assembly of God Church that she was able to make it through her other difficulties. It had devastated her when my father decided to leave her, harder still when he ridiculed her for becoming *religious*. But Mamma loved the move of the Holy Spirit in our church so much that she was willing to take the abuse of my father so she could be in the presence of the Lord Jesus Christ at church. Thankfully, she engendered in me that love for the Holy Spirit.

In spite of my father's malicious behavior toward her, my mother remained stalwart in regard to her children and successfully adapted herself to become both father and mother to us. She felt sorry for me that I had been deprived of a loving father and I felt disappointed for her that she had been deprived of a good, loving husband.

As I grew older, I was determined to be her provider and a good son. I saw how hard my mother worked at the local nursing home just to pay the rent and buy groceries for us, and how she refused to miss a service at the Eighth Street Assembly of God Church. I knew I had to give back to her some of what she had given to me. I wanted desperately to please her. I even recall telling her over and over one day, "Mamma, I'm going to be a preacher. You watch, Mamma, when I get big, I'm going to be a preacher." She laughed and gloated at the possibility. Little did we know the truth of my childhood ambition.

Heavy Hearts

We lived in that small frame house on 50th Street until I was twelve years old. I have only heavy memories of that house—it felt oppressive, strange, and unsettling, almost demonic. To this day, I can feel the pain and gloominess of that place. I still wake up some nights with frightening dreams of feeling trapped there. Maybe it is because my father moved in and out of our lives so much while we lived there, bringing so much grief with him, fighting with my mother yet trying to make it work and trying not to succumb to his restlessness. By the time I was twelve, he decided he just could not make it after all and he left us for good, divorcing my mother. I rarely ever saw him much after that until I was married and had children of my own.

When I turned twelve, I found little incentive for living. The God who claimed to be my father that hot afternoon four years earlier seemed far, far distant from me now. Though I was never suicidal, I had become lethargic about life, indifferent about anything that seemed to matter to my mamma or anyone else. Yes, I still wanted to please her because I knew how much she loved me; but the pain of being abandoned by my father had made me bitter and insecure. We knew he was never coming back now and it made me a sad young boy. It broke my heart to think that after all those years it had come to this and my daddy had never even given my mamma a wedding ring. Life after that seemed hardly worth living.

One evening, a neighbor told a relative that she had seen my father's car in front of a woman's house across town. When my mamma found out, we drove over to the woman's house. It was about one o'clock in the morning by the time we found the place and I'll never forget the look of hopelessness in my mother's eyes when she saw daddy's car in that woman's driveway. It was true that my father had in fact left my sweet little mamma for another woman. She didn't want to believe it, so when we got back to our house, she stayed up the rest of the night going over every address in the Columbus phone book until she finally matched the address to the woman's name where my daddy's car had been. Mamma and I sobbed at the aching reality that my father would never again come home to us. He was gone for good.

Not long after that painful incident, I was playing ball in a sandlot not far from our house on 50th Street. I was having a great time that afternoon. My friends and I were hitting, throwing and catching an old beat-up softball. Before long, I saw my father's car drive up. For months we had had no idea where Daddy was and now I was as surprised as anyone to see him come around. He got out of the car and motioned me over to the fence where he stood with another woman beside him. They were laughing and hugging and acting as if everything in the world were wonderful.

"Son," Daddy said, "I want you to meet someone; this is my new wife."

The words hit me hard in the gut, like a wild-pitch fastball. My eyes shifted from him to her and then in an agonizing slow motion focused on the glittering object on the strange woman's left hand. I was speechless.

My father interrupted my temporary stupor. "Well, aren't you going to say, Hello?" Tears welled up in my eyes as my bottom lip began to quiver. Softly, and without ever looking at him, I mumbled only a single sentence: "You never gave Mamma a wedding ring."

After that fateful afternoon at the sandlot on 50th Street, my father and I seldom spoke.

A Father's Words

It was not easy growing up minus the luxury of a constant, loving father. I longed for the blessing of a daddy and hoped someday to experience that relationship. In fact, shortly after I was called into the ministry, I picked up the telephone to tell my own daddy, "Guess what? The Lord has called me to preach."

I was excited and anxious about what God was going to do in my life. I wanted to share this fantastic news with my father; but instead of enthusiasm and encouragement, there was a long pause of silence and then, "I'd rather see you dead than with a Bible under your arm." He seemed so harsh and cruel. I was shattered inside.

Though it was very painful at the time, it did not matter to me that my father was unsupportive of my decision to enter the ministry. Thankfully, he did eventually accept Jesus Christ as his Savior a few years before his death in 1985, but Daddy always had a difficult time living for God. He spent most of his life struggling through marriages. He was a handsome man and I think perhaps that is why he always had trouble with so many women. (He married seven times. My mamma was his fifth wife and she did not know it until after she married him!) Unfortunately, the devil really had a heyday in my father's life.

Today, as a forty-five year-old pastor, I look back and realize that there was a lot of demonic activity going on. I know very little about Daddy's own upbringing, even though I was in contact with him off and on throughout my life. He simply never opened up to me about his own childhood, and to my knowledge, he never experienced the full blessing and joy of being adopted into God's family. Sadly, my father, unlike myself, never experienced the blessings of being baptized by the Holy Spirit, of knowing the Lord as his Heavenly Father and of being used for God's glory and purposes. The fact that revival broke out at Brownsville Assembly of God on Father's Day is an extra sweet blessing from God to me.

That hot Georgia afternoon, God had spoken to my eight year-old heart. He said that He would be my father. Now I was about to find out that this Heavenly Daddy was one who always kept His promises.

Chapter Two

Hearing the Call

When I think of my growing up years, I remember a lot of pain and insecurity that came to me because of my father's absence. Like any adolescent boy, I was trying to find affirmation and identity, and since my father was never around much to instill those qualities in me, I was willing to look anywhere to find them. Like everyone else, I wanted to feel good about myself. Thankfully, I had a mamma who took me to church so consistently that I did not have much time to look many other places. Besides, I didn't mind going to church since I enjoyed it.

My oldest sister, Shirley, had married a young minister named Paul Wetzel, who was a wonderful Christian. I loved Paul and admired his faith and confidence. He became a big brother to me as well as a great positive influence. Paul's father was the pastor at Riverview Assembly of God in Columbus, not far from where we lived. To a twelve year-old restless boy, Riverview was a chance for me to do something different, even if it did require attending church twice a week.

Because I talked often with my mother about life, she knew how disillusioned and aimless I felt. Maybe that is why we started attending Riverview so much. She had become anxious about me and decided to take me to the doctor to see if there were any problems. All he did was give me nerve pills, but they never really helped because I was not nervous. I just did not have much incentive to live. Maybe Mamma figured that if a doctor could not help my situation, church at least could not hurt it. She was right.

Between my mother's persistence and Paul and his father's influence, I started enjoying church and life more and more. I accepted Jesus Christ as my personal Savior and soon started telling people how I wanted to be a minister. The more we went to church, the more I wanted to learn about God and His ways. I was getting hungry for spiritual food. Now, I had a reason for living!

Godly Examples

By the time I was fourteen years old, I was actively participating in many of the events at Riverview Assembly of God. Godly men and women at the church started talking consistently about this thing called the Baptism of the Holy Spirit. They spoke of its power and importance in helping us know God better. It was all new to me but the Baptism seemed like an exciting part of the Christian life and if it meant getting closer to God, I wanted it.

On Tuesday nights, some of the men of the church would gather together with some of us young boys just to pray. They were determined to instill in us godly principles and to teach us the value of praying consistently. They also made certain that any of us who wanted to learn more about the Baptism of the Holy Spirit could. They offered to pray for any of us who wanted to be baptized in the Spirit.

Each week, I looked forward to Tuesday night prayer times with these men. They taught me to go to God with every concern I had and to be steadfast in God's presence. Their consistency and willingness to meet with us young boys impressed me and I knew I wanted to be like these men some day. Although I didn't fully recognize it at the time, these godly men helped to lay a foundation for me in prayer that would last throughout my life. Their early influence would make all the difference in the world years later when I would have the privilege of pastoring a revival at Brownsville Assembly of God in Pensacola, Florida.

Hearing God's Audible Voice

One Tuesday, I was so excited about prayer service that night that I was having trouble concentrating in school. I had thought about it for weeks and finally decided that I wanted these men to pray over me so I could receive the Baptism of the Holy Spirit. I could not think of anything else that day but what I was hoping to receive later that night at church.

I'll never forget sitting in biology class at about ten o'clock in the morning at Arnold Junior High School. Because we were seated alphabetically, the film projector was right next to us "K's" in the center aisle. We were watching a film on dissection and, while all the other students were either sleeping or really intrigued by the bloody procedure on the screen, I was praying.

"Lord," I prayed silently, "I can't wait to get prayed over tonight for the Baptism. Tonight, please fill me with the Holy Spirit. Please, Lord, fill me." I had been hoping and praying about it for a while but had not yet felt God's power descend on me. I longed for the Spirit's infilling more than ever before.

At that point, it seemed like someone reached over to the projector knob and lowered the sound. When that happened, I jumped, startled by the decrease in the audio. I looked at the movie and saw that it was still going but I could not hear the sound very well. Just then I heard an audible voice come into my left ear and I knew it was the voice of the Lord. Why? Because he called me by my first name, John. I had always been called by my middle name, Alton. While growing up, I never heard anyone refer to me as John. I just knew this was the voice of God speaking to me.

"John, this day I have called you to preach My Word," He said to me. "I want you to stay away from the other boys and girls in your neighborhood who would be a bad influence in your life. Don't go with them. If you do, I'll lose you."

I could not move. The Lord spoke these things so clearly that I had to listen. He went on to tell me other things He wanted to do in my ministry and in the duration of my life, (some of which I have only recently seen come to pass in 1995, some thirty years later). Then He whispered a final word to me that morning in biology class: "This day I will confirm My call in your ear so you will never doubt My word."

The projector sound came right back up at that point and though I did not feel any differently, I knew God had just called me, right there in biology class watching a film on dissecting a frog. I could not believe it. Of all places, why hadn't this happened in prayer meeting tonight? But it didn't matter—I knew the Lord had called me at that moment and I was thrilled.

When the bell rang and I got up to walk out of class, my legs were moving but I could not feel anything. The only way I knew I was walking was because of the movement of my head. It felt just like I was gliding as I walked up the incline of the hall to my math class. When I walked into math class, I saw Mr. Chaplain, a substitute teacher who was a retired Baptist pastor. I went to my seat and just hid behind my books, aware that God had just visited me in a special way.

Before class started, though, Mr. Chaplain looked at me and said, "Alton, come here. What's happened to you?" I thought this was the confirmation the Lord had spoken of, but it was not, I found out later. "Why? What do you mean?" I asked him. Mr. Chaplain explained to me that my face was glowing with the glory of God. I looked different, he said. I started to sob when I heard what he had just said. Then I told him what had happened to me in biology class, that God had called me to preach His Word. When Mr. Chaplain heard this, he started to weep for me, too. I don't exactly remember what happened next, but I don't think we studied much math that morning.

The Donut Lady

I went through the rest of the day stunned and excited that God would speak to me so clearly at school. I could not wait to tell my mamma. When the final bell rang at 3:25, I ran home to find her. I bolted up the steps, threw open the screen door and yelled, "Mother, come here. Mother, come here." Slowly, my mother emerged from the back of the house into the living room where I was throbbing with excitement.

"Mamma, sit down. I want to tell you something important," I said to her. To my surprise, she said, "No, Son, you sit down. I want to tell you something important." "But, Mamma," I exclaimed. "This is important." "No, Son, you need to sit down and listen to me, now." I obeyed.

Mamma then started to tell me what had happened to her that morning. "Today, a woman came by the house before lunch," Mamma began in a soft, serious voice. "She was selling donuts for her church. I didn't know her and she didn't know me. She certainly didn't know I had any children. But she knocked on our door and asked if I wanted to buy some donuts. I went to the back of the house to get a dollar, came back and paid her. We talked for a moment and then she started to leave." Mamma stopped for a second and looked straight into my eyes.

"Son, then this woman stopped on the porch, set the remaining donuts on the edge of the banister and raised her hands into the air. The Holy Spirit spoke through her and said to me, 'This day I have called your son into the ministry to preach My Word. You are to keep him away from the children in the neighborhood who would have a bad influence on him.'" My eyes grew big. Mamma went on to tell me everything God had spoken through this woman; it was exactly what He had said to me in biology class that morning! At that moment, we both knew what I was to do with my life and neither of us have ever doubted since God's calling for my life in the ministry came.

That night I had a prayer service like I had not had before. I received the Baptism of the Holy Spirit and realized fully the call God placed on my life. Now what I needed was specific training and discipleship from a godly man. It became clear to me that I was going to need a firm foundation because in proportion to the way God calls a person is usually in proportion to the way he will suffer. My call was serious and exciting; suffering would surely follow. Life was not going to get any easier for me just because I now knew God's direction and desire for my ministry. It would take an incredible man to mold in my young life a foundation that could not be shaken in the coming years. I found that man in *Pastor Raymond C. Wetzel.*

Chapter Three

A Godly Influence

The first time I saw Pastor R.C. Wetzel, I was afraid. My sister Shirley had married his son Paul when I was only five years old. To a young boy, Pastor Wetzel's jet black curly hair, his raspy *preacher's voice* and the limp he walked with (a result of a childhood bout with polio) were frightening. So, I watched him from a safe distance.

As I grew older, I kept watching him. I watched him preach on Sundays at Riverview Assembly of God church in Columbus. I listened to him pray during the week. And mostly, I watched him interact with people with such kindness and love that I began to understand what it meant to be a Christian man. Even though he was my oldest sister's father-in-law, he was more than just another family member to me. He was a preacher.

By the time I was fourteen years old, my spiritual teeth had been cut and there was no turning back for me. I knew I was called of God to preach and nothing was ever going to change my mind. Now I needed to do whatever was necessary to grow in the ways of God. Because God had already confirmed my calling to my mother in such a remarkable way, she agreed that I was ready for special training and spiritual preparation. So when Brother Wetzel approached her about disciplining me, she was more than willing to let him invest his time in my young life.

Every week, this man would gather a group of us teenage boys who felt called into the ministry. We would sit, eager to learn, in a Sunday school room at Riverview Assembly of God as he taught us the Scriptures. I will never forget how, week after week, this tall, stately man would teach a specific Bible lesson for one full hour to this scraggly group of teenage boys, and then ask us questions about it to make sure we understood the spiritual principles. When we answered correctly, he would call us up to the chalkboard one by one. For the next hour, he expected us to recite back to him the same lesson he had just taught. We could not leave until we each had the opportunity to teach him. It was a powerful way to learn the Bible and the skills for teaching it. When I attended Bible college three years later, I found I already knew many of the Scriptures because of Brother Wetzel's instructions.

In addition to these weekly teaching sessions, Brother Wetzel would gather any of us who wanted to join him at the church for midnight prayer meetings. Every single night for the next two years, this pastor met with us and some of the other men at the church to pray. Because Columbus was a mill town, some of the men used to get off work around 11 P.M. and come to the church to pray late at night. We had all kinds in those late night prayer meetings. We had the kind who would pray aloud and bang the altars. I could hear them all over the church. Then we had the quiet type who would lift their voices gently as they prayed. All were godly men I greatly admired.

Ours was a tumultuous time in American·

history: the Civil Rights Movement was just beginning in our country so our little town in Georgia was feeling the tension of this significant struggle for equality. This, along with specific concerns for his flock, motivated the pastor to call for nightly prayer at Riverview. I was eager to join him.

Restoration Begins

Just as my father had left painful wounds in my heart, Brother Wetzel's godly influence and discipleship began to restore it. When he prayed for me to be baptized, it changed my life. I was young enough, vulnerable and, impressionable enough that I believe God put him into my life to reverse the damage that had been done in earlier years; and he really did. That dark cloud I felt so often in the house on 50th Street began to lift.

Hope came into my life, and Brother Wetzel nurtured in me an excitement about the ministry that remains with me to this day. In many ways, he became an anchor to me, a mentor in the best sense of the word. I have always had a strong sense of people and the more I spent time with this man of integrity, the more I knew that he was a humble, godly man; the type I hoped to be like, someday, but I also wasn't naive. I knew Brother Wetzel had a brilliant German mind and was smart enough and talented enough to be working a thousand other jobs anywhere he wanted. Instead, he chose to take a handful of teenage boys and pour his life into us. He was a virtuous man, full of integrity, strength and wisdom.

Imagine my concern, then, when I discovered Brother Wetzel was thinking of leaving our church. I was almost sixteen years old when he found out that a small group of people in the church were turning against him. Though everyone knew what a wonderful man of God he was, some members were wanting to get a preacher who was a little more social, and a little more dynamic than Brother Wetzel.

One Sunday night, several of us went to eat a hamburger at the little cafe on Second Avenue. We sat and talked and I could tell the pastor's heart was burdened. That's when he told us he was thinking of resigning because he did not want to be in the middle of a church fight. He would not compromise his personal convictions to become the type of preacher he thought these people wanted and so he was considering leaving us altogether to pastor a church in Peninsula Florida. I was determined to pray all the more as we headed back to the church.

A Night to Remember

Though we had been praying together every single night for almost two years now, this particular Sunday night prayer gathering was particularly ponderous. The events in our town and the division in our church were beginning to take their toll on our spirits. There had been numerous race riots not far from the church and our little building had been broken into more than once. Air conditioners and office equipment had been stolen. Someone had been shot and wounded right outside earlier that week. We were weary. We needed God to strengthen us. Thus we gathered that night in our usual routine. Brother Wetzel taught us from the Word, then we taught him. Next, we began praying.

It was almost midnight as we walked around the church interceding for our church, our families and our friends. But with the external circumstances being what they were, police coming by every hour or so to check on the church to make sure each door was securely locked, tonight's prayer time was especially difficult.

Our church was an old style building with a near twenty-five foot high ceiling. We had doors with two slip bolts at the top and the bottom. In all there were five locks on the front door.

The street lights from outside streamed through the windows in the sanctuary so we kept the main lights off as we prayed. I was struggling to keep focused on prayer that night. I looked around the sanctuary and could see the blonde, flat top haircut of one of the church men, Junior Kirkland. He was about six foot, six inches tall and was moving slowly around the building praying. I also could see the white long sleeve shirt of Brother Wetzel as he knelt in his usual corner.

"Well, boys," I finally heard Mr. Kirkland say. "I think I'm going to put my shoes on and go home." I thought to myself, thankful for the excuse to get home as well, that it had been a hard, laborious prayer time that night and I was just plain tired. I saw that big figure of a man move toward the altar bench and slowly put on his shoes. Then, he sat straight up, and without ever saying a word, every other man and boy made his way to the front altar benches as well. Everyone was silent as suddenly an air of expectancy filled the room as Brother Wetzel finally made his way to sit with us. We sat completely still. Then a holy hush came over us in unison, flooding the church. I felt a hallowed quiet blow over everyone in the building.

All of a sudden, both of the sanctuary doors flung open, doors I knew had been bolted and locked. I can still hear the loud pop of the tin door knob hitting the plaster walls. All seventeen of us looked up to see two powerful looking angels walk through the entrance. One turned like a soldier and went to the right side in the back of the sanctuary and stood there solemnly, filling that area from the floor to the ceiling.

Right after him, the other marched by, turned like a soldier and went to the left side of the church. He, too, stood solemnly, his presence reaching from the floor to the ceiling. They were beautiful and tranquil as they stood before us at attention. My eyes shot from left to right and out through the foyer where the doors were wide open. I could see cars going by outside; their headlights were as bright and real as the two standing in the sanctuary.

This is not a vision, I thought to myself. I'm really seeing this. "Dear God," I prayed, "I shouldn't be here. I'm too young for this." Though we had prayed nightly for two years, I had not seen anything like this before and I was not sure what to do. I glanced at the other men and boys and their wide open eyes confirmed for me that they were seeing what I was seeing. I knew this wasn't a vision. We were standing on holy ground!

When I looked back at one of the angels, I noticed no wings or shields or helmets. I simply saw different hues of blues, pinks, and golden brilliant colors forming an aura around them that was too bright to pierce. They stood radiantly for what must have seemed like the longest five minutes I'd ever experienced. It was clear that they were standing guard over the church. Then, as if they got an order, they turned like soldiers, marched back to the middle aisle and right out the door toward the passing cars outside.

We sat in silence, stunned. No one moved.

Finally, Brother Wetzel slowly stood, and walked toward the back of the church to close the doors. Like little children fearing for their safety, each of us followed on his heels as he made his way to the doors. When we got back to the area where they had been, we all fell like dominos under the power of the Spirit, a power so strong we were unable to stand. Those doors were still open and nobody bothered us all night long. At three o'clock in the morning we were as safe as we could be, cradled in the arms of God's holy creatures.

The next thing I knew the sun was coming up, streaming through the sanctuary windows like the street lights had six hours before. As we awoke, we noticed the doors were still wide open. They were a reminder of our heavenly visitors and a testimony to God's promise to watch over us and guard us through the night.

What followed in the next service was an answer to the pastor's prayers. With seventeen men having seen the angels in the church, they could not keep quiet. Everyone knew about the angels, but what happened at the midweek service was yet another miracle.

Things seemed ordinary at the start as the pastor began to pray, just before the offering. We bowed our heads but as the first words came out of his mouth, the entire church fell under the power of the Holy Spirit. Thirty-eight people, many of whom had been coming to church for years, received the baptism of the Holy Spirit. God's Spirit fell on that place and our little Riverview Assembly of God Church was never the same.

From that point on, Brother Wetzel never heard another complaint or whimper out of any member. His spiritual authority had been restored, verified through the power of prayer, and the divisiveness in our church had been dealt with.

Brother Wetzel told us later that the Lord had spoken to him that glorious night about not going to Florida. He was to stay here and multiply himself in us teenage boys. "If you do that," God told him, "You will reach more people through these young preachers

than you ever could have reached on your own."
Thankfully, Pastor Wetzel obeyed.

Eulogy of a Saint

Imagine the incredible privilege it was for me
to have this man's life poured into mine during the
next twenty five years as I learned to pastor my own
church. Brother Wetzel married me and Brenda and
dedicated our two sons, Scott and John Michael.
Numerous times he even came and preached to my
congregations, encouraging the flock in the same way
he had encouraged us, and challenging us with
Scripture like he had so many times before. My first
taste of God's presence of power and fire was because
of Brother Wetzel. And once you've experienced gold,
you cannot settle for less again.

When I buried this giant for God in 1989, I
thought my heart would break. I was asked by the
family to eulogize this great patriarch of the church
and I did so with a huge lump in my throat and a
sickness inside. Their grief and loss was mine as well.
Brother Wetzel was in a glorious heaven, now, but it
hurt deeply to have to let him go. The night before
the funeral, the Holy Spirit poured this poem into my
heart to honor a man whose individual pursuit of God
had sparked the same passion and thirst in me and in
so many others:

I can still see his prophecy chart
And that ever present pointer
That special place in midnight prayer meetings

That seemed to be his hallowed corner

I can remember how many would take
Advantage of his goodness
They would borrow from him and never pay him
    back
They'd get him to co-sign on loans
And then leave him without a trace or track

He was the most forgiving man
He had the gift of mercy and grace
You could hear it in his voice
And you could see it in his face

I used to wonder is he an angel or a man
In my eyes he was flawless
And his virtues were as
Numberless as the sand

As far as I'm concerned—he was never
Appreciated as I thought he should have been
To overlook his brilliant German mind, his
    insights
And wisdom—is almost a sin

I'm convinced he could have become wealthy
And famous had he really wanted to
But he chose to be a humble servant
And to minister to me and you

Once he had a vision
Or maybe it was a dream
He went up into heaven
On an elevator or so it seems

But suddenly he was spotted
And was commanded to return
It isn't time for you yet, said a
Voice loving yet stern
But before he had to leave, Christ allowed
Him to see many glorious sights

I think he said he heard some beautiful songs
And saw all the beautiful lights
He saw many mansions under construction
Hundreds and thousands not just a few
But suddenly Christ stopped and said, Son
This one is for you
He suddenly realized the purpose of his visit
And knew why he came
Jesus wanted him to see that inscribed
Above his mansion's door was his name

For years after that mysterious visit
I would often hear him say
Alton, my mansion's not quite finished
But it will be one day

When it is, after all's been said and done
I'll enter that magnificent place
When my race has finally been run

Well, his race came to an end
On May twenty-four
I'm convinced if anyone has ever made it
R.C. Wetzel walked through heaven's door

By now he's seen Jesus and has gotten settled in
No doubt he's met old acquaintances

And possibly even made some new friends

I know I've got to close
And pen these few remaining lines
My memories of him are not exhausted
But I've used up my allotted time

The impact on my life
That R.C. Wetzel has made
Was through his ministry and his example
I was saved

No one can ever replace
This pastor, dad and friend
As far as I'm concerned
He is the best there ever has been.

Section Two

Fanning the Flame

*"Thou shalt be visited of the Lord of hosts with...the **flame of devouring fire**."*
Isaiah 29:6

Chapter Four

Learning to Minister

There is no price tag great enough to reflect the value of a godly foundation for the ministry. It is crucial if we are to be effective servants of the Lord. Brother Wetzel's example and influence laid such a foundation for me. He showed me what it meant to be a Christian leader who prays and listens to God. These are qualities essential for pastoring any church and especially a church that experiences a fresh outpouring of the Holy Spirit. I will always be grateful for him.

Of course, I also know that God uses a variety of experiences and people to shape our character and make us more like Him. Because I was called to preach His Word, I knew it was only a matter of time before I would encounter several exciting situations that would prepare me for the Brownsville revival.

After finishing school, I married a beautiful blonde-headed girl named Brenda who I met at Riverview Assembly of God. She was witty, popular, and at first, did not want to have anything to do with this *religion stuff*. She was having too much fun at high school parties; that is, until her mother had a dream that changed her mind.

In the dream, her mother saw Brenda drinking and laughing in a number of beer joints. These places were smoky and loud and Brenda was walking around the bars with a painful limp; a terrible car accident had crippled her. The dream, her mother told her, was God's way of warning her that she needed to start making better choices in her young life, or the dream might become reality. "That's what you'll be like if you don't come to the Lord," her mother said.

"I don't want to hear it," Brenda said rebelliously, but her mother persisted. "God has so much for you, Brenda," she said. Then she surprised the teenager: "God even wants you to marry a preacher, a man full of wisdom so you will be happier than you could even imagine. But it's your choice. He wants you to come to Him."

Shortly after that dream, the energetic cheerleader started attending our church. Soon, she got saved at Riverview and started taking her Christian walk more seriously. She studied the Bible, prayed often with the adults at the church and grew confident in her new relationship with Christ. Her mother, of course, was excited for her daughter's spiritual development. Brenda wanted simply to serve the Lord. That's when I knew I had to marry her. She has been my faithful partner in the ministry ever since.

By the time I turned twenty, I was working as a lab technician at the Water Works in Columbus, Georgia. Brenda and I had a new baby, a new home, and a new car. My boss encouraged me often on the job, feeling I had great potential in the company. Life was going well for Brenda and me, and we were eager to serve God in whatever ways He showed us.

One weekend we ran into Aaron Wall, the District Superintendent for Georgia's Assemblies of God. "When are you going into the ministry, John?" he asked me as soon as he saw me. I was content at the Water Works, earning a good salary, enjoying the challenge of the job. But I tried to sound spiritual and so I answered, "When God opens the door."

"There's a church in Vidalia open right now that needs a pastor," he surprised me. "I'll have a deacon call you about it." True to his word, I got a call from a deacon that night and the next Sunday I was preaching at the Vidalia First Assembly of God. On the spot, they voted ninety-nine percent in favor of making me their new pastor. I knew I had to accept. This was God's open door for me to preach His Word; but I still had to go to the Water Works the next day.

My boss called me into his office early that Monday morning. I was nervous knowing I had to resign my position. He was smoking a cigar when he announced to me: "I've got great news for you, Kilpatrick. The city likes you. You're about to get the largest raise of any other employee. They'll even pay for you to finish college. Congratulations." I trembled.

"Mr. Hudson, I appreciate it so much, but I've got to resign," I told him. He looked at me like I had two heads. "I've been called into the ministry and was just offered a position as pastor at a church in Vidalia. I'm sorry." "You're a fool," he mumbled as he walked out of the office. He was probably right, I thought.

Two weeks later as I left the Water Works, I walked out to our little Volkswagon and stood still for a moment, looking at the plant. "Lord," I prayed, "I don't know what it is going to be like in the ministry, but I make a pledge to you that I won't ever go back into a secular job." How could I? God had called me to preach.

Stepping Stones

I could not have asked for a better church as a first time pastor than Vidalia Assembly of God. The small congregation of forty people was comprised of faithful, caring souls who loved God with all their hearts. They were willing to risk hiring me and committed themselves to praying for me often.

Now, Vidalia was not a big city; it was known only for onions and for the headquarters of the Piggly Wiggly grocery store chain. Our people were good, humble, country folks who worked hard for their families (which was a good thing because our little church building was going to need a lot of work).

My first Sunday as the pastor I almost tripped over torn up carpet as I walked to the pulpit. It was a dilapidated building—a little country church that had served its people well. We remodeled the building and Brenda and I stayed there for the next two years, amazed that God would cause our congregation to grow to 125 members.

We then felt called to take a pastoring position

in Warner Robins, another small Georgia town just south of Macon. From 1973 to 1979, we worked with a congregation of 175 at the First Assembly of God church in Warner Robins. Because it was a military town, we were able to build relationships with wonderful people from all over the world. Our second son was born there, and I saw Christian character in godly people like I hadn't before.

I believe God sent us there to teach us about Christian integrity. By the time we left, the congregation had grown to 300 and we had grown in character as well. It was difficult to leave; but we felt a special affinity with Pastor Hansel Vibbert at Calvary Temple Assembly of God in Evansville, Indiana. He was retiring and I felt honored to take over the work he had nurtured there for thirty-three years. So we left Georgia and headed for *cold* country.

At Calvary Temple, God gave me experience for the first time with television and cross cultural ministry. I learned more about pastoring, caring for a much larger congregation, and praying faithfully with sensitive people who supported and loved me.

Again, we watched our membership grow, this time from 650 people when we first arrived to over 1,000 by 1982. Calvary Temple, like the other churches, was a significant landmark for me. It was God's way of confirming to me that our steps had in fact been ordered of the Lord. I loved Calvary Temple and had no intention of leaving; but, as always, God had different plans. We were following in his footsteps and now He had a new place for us to go.

Returning South

One day I called my sister, Shirley, at her home in the Florida panhandle. We chatted about the ministry, our families and how God was working in our lives. Shirley was concerned for her community. She told me, "John, what Pensacola needs is a good church like Calvary Temple. In fact, I think there's a church here that needs a pastor." Though she and Paul were living and pastoring in Jay, Florida (forty miles North of the Pensacola Area), she was convinced that there was a great need in Pensacola. "I'm not interested," I told her; but as we hung up, I could not get her comment out of my mind.

Two days later, the board from Brownsville Assembly of God in Pensacola contacted me and asked if I would be interested in serving as their senior pastor. Our church in Indiana was doing so well that the thought of another move was far from appealing. Still, I agreed to go down and visit with them.

Now, I was torn. I sought God's direction and sensed Him saying, "Go and I will bless you. Stay and I will bless you." It was that simple. So Brenda and I drove to Pensacola and even before we pulled into the church parking lot, we knew God's Spirit was moving. The board introduced us to the legacy of Brownsville Assembly of God, a church started in 1939 by a group of godly men and women concerned about bringing the good news of Jesus Christ to Pensacola.

We were impressed with the vision of these people, moved by their character, and, mostly, attracted to their desire for the movement of the Holy Spirit. Because we had had such wonderful churches in the past, we recognized that these, too, were godly people who wanted deeply to know God, and who honored their former pastors with dignity and respect. Although the church was located in what was considered by some to be a *bad* part of town, (the Brownsville area had been on the decline for several years), we could still see God's hand on this congregation of 300. We believed this to be God's doing so we accepted the board's invitation.

We left Evansville, Indiana, on Valentine's Day, 1982. I preached my first Sunday at Brownsville Assembly of God one week later. For the next ten years, we watched God move in a variety of ways: a television ministry was started, a soup kitchen and other outreach ministries were initiated. People got involved in all types of ministry, from prayer groups to outreach efforts to evangelistic Bible studies. Attendance increased, our pastoral staff was expanded, families came, individuals grew. It was a marvelous work of God to watch; but it did not stop there.

Because of the growth, we started to recognize the need to enlarge our facilities. It did not make sense for us to pluck up our roots and move to another part of town. Instead, by 1989, we went to work on building a new, larger sanctuary on the west side. Someone asked me why we did not just move out of *this neighborhood* altogether. I thought it was apparent: the community is not here to change the church, the church is here to change the community. We decided to stay put and pray that God would provide according to His will.

For the next three years, we focused most of our prayers and resources on constructing the new church building. It required all my energy and attention. Little did I know God cared more about building a house of prayer than He did a new sanctuary made of bricks and mortar.

Chapter Five

Building a House of Prayer

Our new church building was finished and ready for dedication in January of 1991. That same week, the Gulf War broke out. Many were prayerful as the fighting continued but when the U.S. claimed quick victory in the war, Americans promptly went back into their attitude of self-sufficiency. When America gets back in that mindset, the church often follows suit. Our church was no different.

Attendance at the *new* Brownsville Assembly of God was good; we had good crowds, good services, and everyone seemed happy about the new changes. We were enjoying success. Why, then, was I feeling so empty, like something was missing? Maybe it was the unfortunate fall of so many well-known Christian leaders still taking its toll on me. Perhaps it was the weariness and emotional let down brought on by three years of intensive planning, constructing, and financing our new building. Or possibly it was the reality that the challenge, the drive, was over and I was not sure what to look forward to now. When by all accounts I should have been on top of the world, I found myself struggling with the Lord, telling Him, "This doesn't feel like it did when I was a boy coming up in Riverview."

I wondered, "what in the world is going on in my life?" As a result, I knew I needed to take a good hard look and evaluate who I was as a pastor and basically who was I as a Christian man.

For the next two years, I searched my soul and sought God in new ways. Soon, I was spending more time alone with Him, especially on Saturdays in the church sanctuary as I prepared for Sunday services. I was hungry for His Word, willing to try anything to get closer to God, and hoping with all my heart that He would show me more of Himself. I could not stop thinking of my early foundational years of intimacy with Jesus that Pastor Wetzel had taught me. I longed for more of the same.

By August of 1992 and through September, I decided that instead of preaching at our Sunday night services, I would pray for anyone who wanted to receive the baptism of the Holy Spirit. That first night, over 100 people came forward to receive the baptism, and many more came forward for specific prayer. The next Sunday night was equally as powerful a service: more than sixty people received the baptism of God's Holy Spirit. I could sense something was stirring and there was no way I was going to back down now.

The Holy Spirit then began to deal with me about Sunday night services. I admit that I have never been a traditional preacher. I am the first to say that if something is not working, don't put it in the Intensive Care Unit. If it is dying, I say let it die. If God wants to resurrect something, He can. So instead of coming back on Sunday nights and trying to duplicate a Sunday morning service, God began to remind me of the Scripture, *"My house shall be called a house of prayer," Matthew 21:13.*

I started to see that if I took a pie gauge of

everything that was being done in our church and broke that pie up, prayer was usually the thinnest slice. The biggest slices of the pie were the preaching, the worship, the offering, and a little bit of altar time when we prayed with people. The Holy Spirit showed me that though His house was supposed to be a house of prayer, ours was really everything but prayer. Something had to change.

A Banner Strategy

Soon I began to understand that God wanted our Sunday night services to be totally dedicated to prayer; but I needed a strategy. While praying, I felt led to divide the church into segments and use specific banners simply as categories to help direct our prayers. As a result, we organized a committee led by long-time member Jennifer Colley to begin working on original designs for the specific prayer banners. Isaiah 31:8 proclaims *"even the princes of the enemy were terrified at the sight of the banner of the Lord being raised."* So our banners were carefully created to give glory to God and bring unity among our people. They were not to be religious icons or spiritual symbols; they were simply to represent a category of prayer that people could rally around, similar to a sign or poster at a political campaign.

What happened next was another indication to me that something great was stirring in the wings. As God gave Moses twelve tribal leaders to assist him in leading the people, I believe the Holy Spirit gave me twelve categories of prayer for the banners so that everyone in the church would feel included: there was to be a warfare banner; a family banner; a souls banner; one for the leaders of our country; a healing banner; a banner for pastors; one for the peace of Jerusalem; a schools banner; a Brownsville Assembly of God ministries banner, and, of course, a banner for revival. Later we added a children's banner and eventually a banner for survivors of catastrophes (such as earthquakes, floods and tragedies.)

Each banner had a scripture embroidered on it along with its name and a pictorial representation of each theme. The banners took months for our ladies to make and they had to be large enough for our new sanctuary. We had no idea to what extent God would use them. We just believed with singleness of heart that they were to be made.

When the time came to display the various committee's handiwork at a Sunday night prayer service, we had a large crowd of about 1,000 people. One by one, the banners were brought out and marched through the sanctuary. Our worship minister, and the rest of the team, led us in praise and worship songs. I noticed as each particular banner was presented, some people would start to cry when they saw it. I wondered what was going on. Before then, I had been wondering how to divide evenly the congregation into segments to pray around these banners. I contemplated dividing the people alphabetically and asking them to pray around each one. But I was afraid some banners would be overwhelmed and others would be scarce.

Nonetheless, as the banners were paraded through the sanctuary that night and relevant worship songs were played accordingly, I again noticed certain people would begin to cry when they would see certain banners. I scratched my head and thought to myself, "How strange to see people weep and cry at the sight of a specific banner."

When the banner for the leaders of our country was brought in, I was riveted by its presence. To my surprise, I began to cry. I lost all composure—something I seldom did in public and rarely at home even with my own family. I broke down and wept for the leaders of our country. I buried my head in my hands and started sobbing, and when they saw their pastor weeping, most of the church did the same.

Finally, after all the banners were displayed throughout the sanctuary, I wiped my eyes long enough to follow the Holy Spirit's leading: I was to encourage the congregation to go to the banner that they had cried over. As soon as I made that announcement, everyone got up and joined others around a particular banner. No one was left in his or her pew and the people around the banners were evenly distributed. Prayers were lifted up that evening as our congregation set a precedence of intercessory commitment that continues weekly to this day.

No Easy Task

That first year of Sunday night prayer services around the banners, as exciting as it was, was no easy task for me. It was as if a demon on my shoulder would start to taunt me, telling me things would change if I were not careful. "You're going to lose your crowd if you keep this prayer stuff up," it seemed he whispered in my ear. "How many people are going to come to church on a Sunday night just to pray? You are crazy."

Each Sunday night, I was on pins and needles as I charged the people after the praise and worship to go to their banners to pray. I kept fearing they were not going to keep coming. I debated with myself. Who is going to make the effort to come back on Sunday nights just to pray? They could go home where they could be resting or go to another church and hear good preaching. Who would want to come back up here just to pray? To my amazement, our church grew over twenty percent on Sunday nights.

People began to make comments to me like, "I am so thankful I know I'll have a set time to pray this week," or "I am so thankful I can start my week by coming to pray on Sunday night and get ready for the week to come." Even the children and youth had a place to go during the services as they rallied around their school banners.

I appointed leaders for each banner. The leader would hand out prayer requests as the people would rally around their banners to pray. These leaders would then take five minutes to exhort their people on how to pray specifically for the topic of that banner.

When I wasn't pacing the sanctuary out of

nervousness, I'd go to the banner for the leaders of our country. At that particular time, we prayed for the Surgeon General Jocelyn Elders to be dismissed from office because of the bad example she was setting. Of course, we dealt with that issue specifically with what we called, "pin-pointed, rifle-shooting prayer." From there, we would pray for other difficult issues like the abortion situations here in Pensacola, for President Clinton and his wife, for bills coming up in the Congress, for state and local officials, and other matters of national and international scale.

We would gradually increase worshipful instrumental music in the background to indicate to the prayer leaders when it was time to quit talking about the prayer requests and start praying. As the music got louder, a roar of prayers could be heard going up from the people throughout the sanctuary. And those beautiful blended voices roared their prayers to heaven week after week. Every time I heard that roar of prayers, my spirit would leap within me in a powerful way. About an hour later our prayer time would end and we would come together to share Holy Communion. Every week we partook of the bread of God's presence in fresh, powerful ways.

Evangelist Dick Reuben brought us a series of important messages that I believe were instrumental for laying a corporate foundation for what was to come. Brother Reuben also prophesied just before Easter that revival would fall in our church, and that, as a result, we would have an opportunity to touch the entire world. I knew we were reaching Heaven. God was indeed about to send a *feast of fire!*

A Night to Remember

I will never forget one night as hundreds of people from our congregation were participating in their prayers around the banners. They would pray forty-five minutes or so at one banner and then, migrate to another. As I watched this parade of prayer, I sensed the Holy Spirit say to me, "If they continue to make this house a house of prayer, I will visit it with My glory." I rejoiced. That was the *word* I had been waiting for.

The story of Jesus visiting the temple flashed into my mind. I remembered reading that Christ had to *purify* the temple first. After clearing away all the debris that was not supposed to be there then He could make it a house of *prayer* where people from all backgrounds and circumstances could come to pray.

As the people began to pray, God would turn His house into a house of *power* where He could heal the sick and deliver the troubled in heart. That power would then quite naturally draw praise and thanksgiving from the people, making it now also a house of *praise*. That's when the children came around it crying Hosanna!

So these four steps, *purity, prayer, power and praise,* were essential if we were going to see God's glory revealed. By the time I understood this, a year had passed since our first prayer service. At last I was feeling acclimated to the idea of Sunday night prayer services so much so that I could focus in on one banner for prayer. Before then, I would just walk around the sanctuary because I was so uptight. I wondered if this were how it was going to work. I was not afraid to break tradition, but I was afraid these people would not want to keep coming like this just to pray; but they did. As a result, we as a body were being purified and about to experience a power we could never have envisioned.

Revival in the Wings

Even though we saw many prayers answered during these Sunday night services, we saw that there began to be more of an emphasis on the revival banner. My wife, Brenda, was the prayer leader for the revival banner and we recognized that each week, people would pay particular attention to it. They would gather around it for long periods of time, seemingly in deep travail and especially intense intercession.

All along I had made it clear that these banners were not icons to be worshipped, that they had no intrinsic power in and of themselves. They were simply symbolic tools to help us pray for specific issues and the revival banner was catching our prayer attention more and more.

Sunday evening prayer was having a profound liberating effect on our private and personal prayer lives. For instance, when I would pray in the church sanctuary on Saturday nights by myself, I would feel such a freedom that I began praying for specific areas that before I would never have thought of. I prayed for an open heaven. I started anointing everything on the platform of the church. Instead of criticizing what was wrong to the Lord, I would pray positively and ask for blessings.

My teenage years of prayer and intercession at Riverview Assembly of God were bearing fruit again in my life, and I was thirsty for God's presence more and more. Like Jacob of old, I was holding out for the blessing I knew God had in store for me and our church.

Chapter Six

Priestly Blessing

I love and enjoy lively church music; but to my disappointment I was never gifted in this area; so like most pastors, I had always dreamed of having a church with an organized ensemble of players. I epecially wanted a band blessed with the clear mellow sound of brass instruments. At Brownsville, things were beginning to come together. We had a few who played and now it looked as though my envisioned orchestra might finally materialize.

When we built the platform in the new sanctuary, I took a step of faith and asked the architects to make space for an orchestra pit. The sunken area, behind the chairs designated for staff pastors, and in front of the choir loft, was perfect—not only for a piano and organ, but large enough for an orchestra, complete with brass section!

In my Saturday times of prayer in the sanctuary, I went to that area. "God," I would begin, "You know I've never had an orchestra in my church. O Lord," I continued, "I need an orchestra. When are You going to give me one? When is our church going to have the wonderful sound of brass instruments You helped man create?"

For weeks I prayed this way for an orchestra. One Saturday, God interrupted. "Son," the Holy Spirit softly asked, "instead of speaking curses, whining, and complaining about your desire for an orchestra, why don't you bless it?"

I was stunned. But as I pondered the content of my praying, I realized God was right. I had been using prayer to complain to God—in effect, "cursing" the situation.

By next Saturday evening, my prayers for an orchestra changed dramatically. Standing in the sunken area, I began anew, "Father, I bless this area. I thank You that one day a tremendous orchestra will fill this space. I thank You that Brownsville Assembly of God is attracting people with new talent, including those who play brass instruments. I bless this area in Your Name, Lord, and say that it is fertile ground for an orchestra."

The Sterile Becomes Fertile

Within 90 days, God answered. When I had pastored First Assembly in Warner Robins, Georgia, my congregation included an Air Force colonel. Through the years—even though he was transferred to another area, and I came to pastor Brownsville—we had kept in touch.

Now a retired Air Force colonel, he called me. "Pastor, I am coming to Pensacola to apply for a job as an R.O.T.C. instructor in your area. That Sunday I am coming to worship at your church. I am also bringing my brass trumpet. Would you like me to play in your orchestra?"

I didn't even know he owned a brass trumpet, much less played one. But he got the job he applied for, and was the start of Brownsville's orchestra—mingling mellow brass tones in our church's exuberant times of praise and worship.

For nineteen years I had wanted and prayed for a church orchestra, with no results. But now, three months after praying blessings instead of complaints, our church had an orchestra.

God had my attention. I already knew that both persistent prayer and our weekly times of holy communion were vital to revival at Brownsville. Now God added the third element of blessing.

Dick Reuben, a dear friend and a Messianic Jewish evangelist, often stated, "When the pattern is right, God's glory falls." I began to understand that blessing was part of God's pattern.

I was already well versed in one reality: there were many sterile, barren areas in our church's life, and in the lives of many people I knew. Often I was struck with the sterility of an empty pew, of sterile situations in people's lives that wouldn't budge to change, of sterile times in our worship services when the Holy Spirit seemed almost absent.

But when I blessed a non-existing orchestra, the sterile had become fertile. As I watched that orchestra grow, so did my own study of blessing in God's Word.

Jesus and Blessing

In His "Sermon on the Mount," Jesus instructs us, "Love your enemies, *bless* them that curse you, do good to them that hate you, and pray for them which despitefully use you, and persecute you" (Matthew 5:44). Blessing was so important to Jesus that He even wanted us to bless our enemies.

In Jewish tradition, an older person blessed a younger person by placing his right hand on the younger person, and speaking words of blessing. Matthew, Mark and Luke all write of parents coming to have Jesus touch or lay His hands on their children; they wanted Jesus to bless their children. Time conscious disciples thought Jesus had better things to do, and rebuked these parents. Then Jesus rebuked the disciples: "Suffer the little children to come unto me, and forbid them not: for such is the kingdom of God'...and He took them up in His arms, put His hands on them, and *blessed* them" (Mark 10:14b & 16).

It was Jesus' desire that everyone be blessed— from the smallest child, to the most undesirable enemy. But Jesus did not stop there.

Jesus gave His very life so you and I can be blessed. Paul clearly stated: "Christ has redeemed us from the curse of the law, having become a curse for us (for it is written, 'Cursed is everyone who hangs on a tree'), that the **blessing** of Abraham might come upon the Gentiles in Christ Jesus, that we might receive the promise of the Spirit through faith" (Galatians 3:13-14, NKJV).

As I studied this verse, I realized afresh that the move of the Spirit I longed for was part of the blessing Jesus died to give me. Blessing was more than important to revival; it was vital.

Blessing in the Old Testament

My growing curiosity about blessing caused me to look further. So I started from Genesis 1, and discovered that God and His people were in the "blessing business" throughout the Old Testament. Even after God completed His crowning creation, man and woman, He blessed them: "So God created man in His own image, in the image of God He created him; male and female created He them. And God *blessed* them" (Genesis 1:27-28a).

Abraham, a man called by God, sent his servant Eliezer to search for a proper bride for his son Isaac. God responded to Eliezer's prayer and he found Rebekah. Rebekah's family was glad for her to find a husband, but slow to let her go. When they finally did, "They *blessed* Rebekah and said to her, 'Our sister, may you become the mother of thousands and ten thousands; and may your descendants possess the gates of those who hate them'" (Genesis 24:60, NKJV). God heard their blessing; Jews today attest to the fact that Rebekah did become the mother of thousands and tens of thousands.

Years later, Isaac's hungry son Esau sold his birthright to his brother Jacob for savory red stew (Genesis 25:29-34). Then, through deceit, Jacob posed as his older brother Esau, and Isaac mistakenly gave Jacob the verbal blessing that should have been reserved for the oldest.

The family head's verbal blessing was a serious matter throughout the Old Testament. That is why "Esau hated Jacob because of the *blessing* with which his father blessed him" (Genesis 27:41a, NKJV). That is why Joseph brought his two sons to Jacob to bless before he died, and why he was concerned when Jacob put his right hand on his younger son, Ephraim, to bless him (Genesis 48); the oldest son was supposed to receive the firstborn blessing, but Jacob reversed that.

That is why orthodox Jews to this day rehearse the blessings Jacob spoke over his twelve sons, "He *blessed* them; he *blessed* each one according to his own *blessing* (Genesis 49:28b). Notice: Jacob did not prophesy over his sons, but he blessed them, speaking over them his desires. And each blessing he spoke came fully to pass, exactly as Jacob spoke it.

Later, kings made a practice of blessing their subjects. After the ark of the Lord was brought to its resting place in the city of David, the king blessed the people: "And when David had finished offering burnt offerings and peace offerings, he *blessed* the people in the Name of the Lord of hosts" (2 Samuel 6:18, NKJV), later distributing to each person a loaf of bread, a piece of meat, and a cake of raisins—perhaps a type of the communion we enjoy today. When King Solomon finished building the Temple, and the ark was in the Most Holy Place, he summoned the people together.

After a lengthy prayer of dedication, King Solomon "stood and *blessed* all the congregation of Israel with a loud voice" (1 Kings 8:55).

Sometimes blessing was and is conditional, as is true with tithing: "Bring all the tithes into the storehouse, that there may be food in My house, and prove Me now in this, says the Lord of hosts, if I will not open for you the windows of heaven and pour out for you such a *blessing* that there will not be room enough to receive it" (Malachi 3:10, NKJV).

Conditional blessing has no effect when the condition is not met. You can push an electric lawn mower when it is not turned on, but tall grass just springs right back up after the mower moves past. But when the condition is met, it is like that electric lawn mower after it is turned on: it devours every blade of grass in its path.

There is a certain mystery about blessing that many still don't understand. But blessing is throughout God's Word, and it remains powerful.

Blessing in the New Testament

Jesus never told us to ask God to bless our enemies, for God cannot bless those with sin. But we're not called to judge sin; Jesus instead told us to bless our enemies (Matthew 5:44). When we refuse to bless our enemies, and harbor hurt, resentment, bitterness or anger, we come in emotional bondage to our enemies. However, when we obey Jesus and bless our enemies, we are freed from that bondage. Maybe this is why Peter said we are "not (to) render evil for evil, or railing for railing; but contrariwise *blessing*: knowing that ye are thereunto called, that ye should inherit a *blessing*" (1 Peter 3:9).

As I studied the New Testament passages, it seemed the believer was to have a lifestyle of blessing: "*Bless* those who persecute you, *bless* and do not curse. Rejoice with those who rejoice; mourn with those who mourn. Live in harmony with one another" (Romans 12:14-16a, NIV).

James found that believers struggle to have a lifestyle of blessing, especially in their speech. He wrote, "For every kind of beasts, and of birds, and of serpents, and of things in the sea, is tamed, and hath been tamed of mankind: but the tongue no man can tame; it is an unruly evil, full of deadly poison. Therewith *bless* we God, even the Father; and therewith curse we men, which are made after the similitude of God.

"Out of the same mouth proceedeth *blessing* and cursing. My brethren, these things ought not so to be. Doth a fountain send forth at the same place sweet water and bitter" (James 3:7-11)?

God was clear in His Word. I then closely watched the words I spoke, especially around my family. Every day I began consciously speaking words of blessing over my wife Brenda, and my sons Scott and John Michael.

My Next Step: Preach About Blessing

My attention soon became fixed on God's words to Moses, outlining how Aaron and the priests were to give blessings to the children of Israel. God told them to say, "The Lord *bless* thee and keep thee. The Lord make His face shine upon thee, and be gracious unto thee. The Lord lift up his countenance upon thee, and give thee peace" (Numbers 6:24-26). The Lord finished His instructions with the words, "And they (the priests) shall put My Name upon the children of Israel; and I will *bless* them" (Numbers 6:27).

In God's Old Testament economy, the priests were responsible to bless the people. But who are the priests in God's New Testament economy? According to Peter, believers are "a holy priesthood" and "a royal priesthood...that you may declare the praises of Him Who called you out of darkness into His wonderful light" (1 Peter 2:5, 9b).

Since we are today's priests called by God to bless others, I felt that I must go beyond studying blessing in God's Word. My next step was to preach about the truth of blessing to my congregation.

In October of 1992, I preached a sermon on "The Power of A Blessing." In that sermon I gave five definitions of blessing: to make whole or holy by spoken words; to ask Divine favor; to wish a person or situation well; to make prosperous; and to make happy or glad.

I also mentioned three things God's Word shows we can bless. First, we can bless situations and circumstances. If there is unsold merchandise at one's job, start blessing it instead of complaining. Secondly, we can bless people, like I was learning to bless my wife and sons. Thirdly, we can bless God, King of Kings and Lord of Lords. As we learn to bless instead of criticizing and complaining in these three areas, we allow God to work more freely in our lives, our attitudes, and our characters.

By January of 1994, I preached the second part of a sermon on "the mystery of blessing." In that sermon I outlined 30 things Scripture indicates we can say in blessing others:

1) God bless you with ability
2) God bless you with abundance
3) God make His angels go with you
4) God give you assurance of His love and His grace
5) God bless you with clear direction
6) God bless you with a controlled and disciplined life
7) God bless you with courage
8) God bless you with creativity
9) God bless you with spiritual perception of God's truth
10) God bless you with faith
11) God bless you with God's favor and with man's favor
12) God bless you with good health
13) God bless you with a good wife or a good husband

14) God bless your hands to bless others
15) God bless you with happiness
16) God bless you with fulfillment
17) God bless you with contentment
18) God bless you with hope and a good outlook on life
19) God bless you with a listening ear
20) God bless you with a long life
21) God bless you with an obedient heart to the Spirit of God
22) God bless you with His peace
23) God bless you with pleasant speech
24) God bless you with a pleasant personality
25) God bless you with promotion
26) God bless you with protection
27) God bless you with provision, safety and strength
28) God bless you with success
29) God bless you with trust and wisdom
30) God bless you with goodness and mercy following you all the days of your life, that you might dwell in the house of the Lord forever.

After I preached about the potential beauty of having parents bless the bride and groom at their weddings, I found myself conducting some moving weddings. I remember when the father and mother stood behind the bride, the father stretching out his right hand on her head, pronouncing blessing on his daughter in the Name of the Lord. After the father and mother of the groom did the same with him, there was not a dry eye in the place.

In one sermon I told of a young Christian man who realized that he had never received a blessing from his aging father. So he went to his unsaved father, and asked that his dad bless him.

His father hesitantly responded, "I guess so, Son. But I don't really know what to do or how to say a blessing."

Since men do not usually express affection to each other, the young man responded by pulling up a chair: "It's not hard, Dad. Just think what you wish would happen with me and my family, and speak those words over me."

As the father began, his words faltered. As his thoughts became clear, his words of blessing for son, daughter-in-law and grandchildren easily poured out. The blessing flowed freely, as did the tears. Father and son bonded that day, and remained close until the father died.

Priestly Blessing

I knew the Lord was pleased that I was teaching the congregation more about blessing. But as I prayed, I also sensed that the Lord wanted me to move beyond preaching and teaching. He wanted me to pronounce blessing on the congregation on Sunday nights, immediately following communion.

Yes, all believers are priests in God's eyes. But God had given me headship of our congregation, and as pastor I was to complete our night of prayer by pronouncing a priestly blessing.

So I searched Scripture again, and composed a final blessing I pronounced at the conclusion of each Sunday night of prayer.

People seemed to enjoy my spoken blessings. I even taught them Jewish custom. The one blessing was to stretch out his right hand as the blessing was spoken; those receiving the blessing were to raise their right hands, symbolic of their desire to receive the blessing.

So at the end of each Sunday night of prayer, I would extend my right hand as they raised their right hands, and pronounced a blessing. On two occasions, after lengthy times in prayer, I forgot about pronouncing the blessing, and dismissed those gathered. Imagine my surprise when they balked and refused to leave. Then, they raised their right hands, prompting me to remember that I still needed to pronounce a blessing over them.

Persistent prayer, weekly "bread of presence" communion, and spoken priestly blessing: three important elements before revival came to Brownsville. Allow me to end this chapter with the written blessing I spoke dozens of times over the Brownsville congregation. And, as you read it, may blessing come to you and your household as well:

"In the Name of Jesus Christ, I bless you with the promises of God which are 'yea and amen.' The

Holy Spirit make you healthy and strong in body, mind and spirit to move in faith and expectancy. May God's angels be with you to protect and keep you.

"Be blessed with supernatural strength to turn your eyes from foolish, worthless and evil things. Instead, may you behold the beauty of things that God has planned for you as you obey His Word.

"I bless your ears to hear the lovely, the uplifting, and the encouraging, and to shut out the demeaning and the negative. May your feet walk in holiness and your steps be ordered by the Lord. May your hands be tender-helping hands to those in need, hands that bless. May your heart be humble and receptive to one another, and to the things of God, and not to the world. May your mind be strong, disciplined, balanced and faith-filled.

"God's grace be upon your home, that it may be a sanctuary of rest and renewal, a haven of peace where sounds of joy and laughter grace its walls, where love and unconditional acceptance of one another is consistent.

"God give you success and prosperity in your business and places of labor as you acknowledge and obey the imperative of Scripture concerning the tithe.

"God give you spiritual strength to overcome the evil one and avoid temptation. God's grace be upon you to fulfill your dreams and visions. May goodness and mercy follow you all the days of your long life.

"The Lord bless thee and keep thee. The Lord make His face shine upon thee, and be gracious unto thee. The Lord lift up His countenance upon you and give you peace.

"I bless you in Jesus' Name."

Section Three

A Feast of Fire

*"And suddenly there came a sound
from heaven as a rushing mighty wind, and
it filled all the house where they were sitting.
And there appeared unto them **cloven tongues
like as of fire**, and it sat upon each of them."*
Acts 2:2-3

Chapter Seven

Revival Falls

One particular Saturday, I had been having trouble with a sprinkler head outside the church. Just before I headed inside for my personal prayer time, I fixed it. I decided to go into the sanctuary through the front of the church and in through the lobby. Usually I had always entered through the back of the church and made my way into the pulpit area to pray. This day, for some reason, I went through the front door of the church. As I entered the lobby, a stack of our bulletins for the next day's service caught my attention. I began glancing through one as I pulled open the door to the sanctuary.

Suddenly, every hair on my arms and neck stood up and my body was chilled from head to toe. It was as if I had walked right into some brilliant power—an angel perhaps—when I opened that door, and I fell up against the side of a pew. It took away my breath. I used the pew to brace myself in the presence of this mysterious power. When I regained my composure, I rushed over to a phone in the sound booth a few feet away to call my wife.

"Brenda, I've just walked into something," my voice quivered and my hands shook as I held the phone. "I don't know what it was, an angel of the Lord or something, but it was powerful." As we hung up, I thought back to that Sunday night at Riverview when we were visited by two angelic beings. Something great had happened then and something great was happening now. Both times, corporate prayer seemed to facilitate it. At Brownsville that night, I went into a wonderful time alone with the Lord. In His sanctuary, I prayed and wept for hours. I fully anticipated a powerful breakthrough at church the next morning but, surprisingly, it did not happen.

The powerful presence I had experienced the night before had not yet descended on us as a corporate body. As a matter of fact, our service was unusually dry. I was disappointed, but I kept returning to the church sanctuary every Saturday night to pray. I sensed and felt the presence of God in powerful new ways. I was a thirsty man in a desert who could not get enough to drink.

At last, I had received the blessing I was personally longing for but strangely enough, our morning church services kept feeling rote and dry. I wondered if our church was going to reject revival, even though they had been more than faithful at our Sunday night prayer services. "Still," I wondered, "are they going to go for it?"

As I began preaching on revival and seeking God again as I had as a teenager, I soon discovered a few members were questioning the direction our church was going. A handful of these members were uncomfortable with our prayer services and my fiery new sermons. This troubled me. My wife and I wanted desperately to experience a fresh move of God's Spirit. Finally, I confessed to God, "If this church does not want a move of Your Spirit, then I'm willing to resign and turn in my keys. I'd rather take a small church of fifty people who want to see God than pastor a church of 2,000 members who might be indifferent."

Once again our congregation surprised me. We were about to experience a Father's Day like we never had. There were some disgruntled members who stayed and went through a terrible struggle as a result. Maybe they just were not ready for it. When the fullness of the flame hit, it was more than they could take. A few put up walls. Eventually, twenty or so left the church altogether but 1,800 others stayed and came together regularly to taste the goodness of God.

Yes, these friends remained, and continue to this day to experience an historical event of a magnitude that none of us could have expected nor anticipated. It happened, I believe, partly because of our commitment to prayer and to coming together to the House of Prayer on a consistent basis.

Still a Struggle

For me, the week prior to Father's Day was nothing short of hell on earth. Thankfully, my own preparation for revival had been based on a sure foundation of regular prayer. I needed to pray so I could receive guidance about new directions, new ways to make our church a better reflection of God's glory. The spiritual principles that I discovered through building a house of prayer provided important preparation for what was about to happen at Brownsville Assembly of God. The wisdom that came from my early years, the decision to pray privately in the sanctuary on Saturday nights, changing our Sunday evening services to prayer meetings, partaking of Holy Communion on a weekly basis, speaking a blessing on the congregation each Sunday night at the close of our prayer service, and the prayer banners all played a part, I believe, in ushering in the revival.

There was no question in my mind that prayer was as central to the revival itself as it was to the preparation of it. Still, even with all the prayer preparation, I was not ready for what proved to be the most hellish week of my thirteen years at Brownsville Assembly of God. There was no way satan was going down without a struggle.

By now, several good friends who were also church members were questioning the direction of our church. Throughout the week, they confronted me with their concerns and disapproval about this new *move of God* our church was expecting. To be honest, it hurt me deeply to hear their comments and I struggled as to why they would not want to be a part of something so wonderful. I tried to reconcile and convince these disgruntled, wary friends that I believed this was really going to be a move of the Holy Spirit. I could not understand why they would be upset about a move of the Holy Spirit coming to our church. But they were afraid we would lose our vision, that we were going to become *weird*. I could only listen. The confrontations were unnerving and humiliating, but God gave me a powerful Scripture verse to console and energize me, *Jeremiah 20:9-11.*

My dear mother also had just died of pancreatic cancer in early May, so I had missed several Sundays in a row at Brownsville being with her before her death. She had supported me at every church I pastored, becoming a member at each. She even moved with us when we went to pastor Calvary Temple in Indiana. Mamma had become a dear friend to my wife and a precious grandmother to our two sons; it was hard to let her go.

When she died, I knew a significant part of me died as well. For the next few weeks, I went through an important grieving process, spending much time in reflection and prayer. As a result, I was absent in the pulpit and feeling derelict in my responsibilities to my congregation. I was aching. I needed to preach on Sunday morning. It would be Father's Day and I hoped things could begin to feel normal for me and the church again.

Fill My Cup

Since we had scheduled my friend of twelve years, Steve Hill, a Texas-based Assembly of God evangelist, to preach at the Sunday night service, Brenda and I met him for coffee on Saturday night. I was looking forward to preaching the next morning and then hearing Steve preach a special sermon at our Sunday night prayer service.

Steve had been radically converted several years before from a tough life of drug addiction and stealing to support his habit. Now he had a heart for evangelism as a result. He was discipled under David Wilkerson and Leonard Ravenhill, and then was involved deeply in the Argentine revival for seven years.

Ironically, Steve also had been feeling spiritually dry in his full-time ministry. He had spent the past three years ministering in South America, Russia, and throughout the United States, and the travel was starting to take its toll. On his way back from Russia, he stopped to rest in England. While there, a Spirit-filled Anglican vicar, whose church was experiencing a powerful move of God, prayed over him.

Steve felt touched and empowered by the Holy Spirit in a new way. His time in England brought great personal renewal for him and he was now ready to watch God move through him. He was excited.

Just weeks before, my wife, Brenda, also had been touched of God after she visited a ministry in Canada. A great renewal of power and joy had fallen on God's people in Canada and I had sent Brenda to go and drink it in. I have to admit I was a little jealous of God's refreshing in both Brenda and Steve, because I was feeling emotionally drained, thirsty for some of the same living water.

When Steve and I met that Saturday night, I told him about the week I had just gone through. I told him that some members had become divisive and concerned, that my heart was still aching at the loss of my mother, and that I was not sure God would really move in our church even though I was committed to preaching on revival. It also felt as if lots of administrative obligations from the week had compounded my weariness. We also had spent every night that week in special meetings with the musical ministry of the McGregors from South Africa. Though I loved and appreciated their ministry, the combined events and busy schedule had left me weary. I was going through a real emotional and spiritual battle.

"I feel beat up," I said to Steve over coffee. "I'm so tired and so worn out, would you preach in the morning? You're excited about the Lord right now, would you preach?" Without blinking an eye, Steve said yes; but neither of us could have anticipated the type of Father's Day we were about to celebrate.

Combustion—The Father's Gift

We arrived early at the church Father's Day morning. Families had lunch plans with their fathers to celebrate the day, so we were expecting a good crowd for both services. We were not disappointed. When Steve got up to preach, he could hardly get through his sermon, he was so excited about the altar call. He kept telling us, "Folks, God is going to move this morning. God is going to move this morning."

I mumbled under my breath, "Yeah, sure, Steve. I've heard this before." Yes, we had been praying for two and a half years that God would bring revival, but I wondered if He really would. Certainly not today when I was so worn down and discouraged.

By the time Steve called the people to come to the altar for prayer for salvation, or for any other need, about one thousand came forward. I walked off to the right side of the platform with Steve to help him pray for the people, but I began to feel a little strange standing next to him as he prayed. Then, I laid my hand on his back and my other hand on a man's head as we prayed for him. The man fell to the ground under God's power; others began to weep or dance or raise their arms in thanksgiving. Some started to shake uncontrollably.

Suddenly, I felt a wind blow through my legs, just like in the second chapter of the book of Acts. A strong breeze went through my legs and suddenly both my ankles flipped over so that I could hardly stand. I thought, "That's weird! O God," I prayed, "What in the world is happening?" I stood on the side of my ankles, unable to get my footing. I literally could not straighten up my feet.

Just then Steve prayed for a woman who fell to the floor under the power of the Spirit. I tried to lift up my legs to step over her but I could not. Finally, I had to ask a friend, Tony Taylor, to come over and help me. He lifted my legs by pulling on my pants and helped me walk back up the platform, step by step. I took the microphone and shouted, "Folks, this is it. The Lord is here. Get in, get in!" I realized God had indeed come, that He had answered our prayers for revival. The *feast of fire* had begun!

Steve walked by me at that point, waved his hand in my direction, and said simply, "More, Lord." I hit that marble floor like a ton of bricks.

Now, I'm as critical as the next person when it comes to things like this. I have seen it all and just don't think I can be fooled. So when I hit that floor and it felt like I weighed 10,000 pounds, I knew something supernatural was happening. God was visiting us. In fact, I lay on that floor from 12:30 through 4 p.m. until some men finally were able to get me up.

It reminded me of the teaching series I had done in church months before on the glory of God. The Hebrew word for glory, *Chabod*, translates *weightiness.* It is like a security blanket. When the first sin happened in the Bible in the garden with Adam and Eve, what lifted off of them was the glory. That is why they knew they were naked; that was *Ichabod*, or *"the glory has departed."*

The heaviness I felt that day, and for the next two weeks, was God's glory visiting us at last. (I think people came those first two weeks just to see Kilpatrick unable to move under God's power! They could not believe that this usually cynical and suspicious preacher was struck motionless. I could barely believe it myself.)

Many families never did make it to celebrate Father's Day dinners with their earthly fathers that afternoon. We had a different kind of Father's Day celebration that lasted throughout the day and then picked up again that evening. It has been going every night since.

The World Watches

Almost every night since that Father's Day service, we have met for revival. The Holy Spirit has manifested Himself in strange and exciting ways, touching all types of people from all walks of life and experiences. About 2,300 or more each night have come to worship God and to receive from Him in His sanctuary. Many have been radically converted; some have been tenderly healed; others have been powerfully renewed. All have drunk deeply of Jesus, *the living water.* It has been a wonder to behold. It has been revival of the Whitfield or Finney type.

After a few months of these nightly meetings, we began to take off Tuesday and Saturday nights to pray and rest, but still felt led of God to meet six times a week until the people stopped coming. Steve had been scheduled to minister in Russia during the Summer, but chose instead to postpone his trip indefinitely, knowing that what began as God's Father's Day outpouring was now something he did not want to miss.

Even the local newspaper, the *Pensacola News Journal* (PNJ) reported on the revival just months after it had begun. The following PNJ story bears witness that, despite what we might think, the world is watching for mighty moves of God. Keep in mind this is from a newspaper printed in 1995 America, not one at the turn of the century when Americans were much more likely to read about spiritual issues in their local newspapers when Charles Finney or Daddy Seymour were leading revivals.

Church experiences divine refreshing-
Thousands continue in weeks-long revival

Believers filled Brownsville Assembly of God with song, praising the presence of the Holy Spirit. 'Let the lost man say I'm found again . . . Let the blind man say I can see again . . . Let the river flow . . . Holy Spirit come.'

Thousands of arms raised. Young and old jumped up and down to music. A teen-age girl collapsed to the floor on her back, her rigid arms raised.

This was the scene on a recent weekday evening, a setting that has been occurring nearly every night at Brownsville Assembly of God Church for six weeks. . . . More than 30,000 people—including visitors from 22 states—have attended church services at the Pentecostal church since the revival started on Father's Day, June 18, said the Rev. John Kilpatrick, Brownsville Assembly of God pastor . . .

. . . Each night, there has (sic) been at least 1,500 first-time attendees, and the 'refreshing from the Lord' has crossed divisions—drawing Jews, Mormons, Baptists, Methodists, Catholics, Episcopalians, independents and other Pentecostals from in and outside the Pensacola area.

'Satan has fought the church so much,' Pastor John Kilpatrick said. 'God's people are worn out, stressed out and burned out. This move of the Holy Spirit, which is happening around the world, is God touching and reviving His people.'

Although Brownsville Assembly of God members

have been praying for such a revival for 2 1/2 years, Kilpatrick has been telling the throngs of Christians: 'This is not a Brownsville thing. This is a God thing.'

Linda B. Smith, program and youth director at Pine Forest United Methodist Church, has been studying revivals since 1968 and started attending the revival on its third day. She's been back more than 12 times.

'A true revival, according to church history, is spontaneous and occurs sovereignly among church people much like spontaneous combustion where the conditions are perfect to create a fire,' she said. 'A revival of this magnitude occurs once, perhaps twice in a century. Pensacola has never seen anything like this.'

And the circumstances are right for a 'spiritual fire,' Smith believes. 'What's happening here lines up with the inner witness of believers. It lines up with church history and it lines up with the scriptures,' she said. ... Bill Langlitz, a Brownsville church member who has attended more than 25 of the services, said: 'The best way to it explain it is God is pouring out his spirit upon all flesh as it says in the Book of Joel in the Old Testament. It started out slowly and then the Holy Spirit started flowing and coming upon the people.'

By word of mouth, the word is spreading about the manifestations of the Holy Spirit, Langlitz said.

Pentecostalism is distinguished by the belief in tangible manifestations of the Holy Spirit, often in demonstrative, emotional ways such as speaking in unknown tongues, falling to the floor, weeping and laughing uncontrollably, shaking and deep bowing.

'There has been uncontrollable, weeping, uncontrollable shaking of the limbs,' Langlitz said.

'And a homosexual named Joseph was transformed—freed from all the filth and garbage of the world.'

Holding her 6-month-old foster child in her arms on a recent evening, Donna Coward lifted one arm in praise and closed her eyes.

'This is like an old-time revival,' she said. 'There has been singing, testimonies, preaching and prayer.'

And there is no end in sight, Kilpatrick said.

'The Holy Spirit is surely visiting Pensacola,' he said. 'I have seen so much unity and support from all denominations. It has blown my mind.'

When revival fell on Brownsville Assembly of God, I had no idea that it would make its way into the local paper, or that a reporter would care about covering it so thoroughly. Or that it would make its way into dozens of other publications and news services with worldwide press. I could never have imagined how exciting it would be for the many people who came night after night, simply feeling spiritually dry, thirsting for a drink from heaven. Their personal stories testify to the goodness of God and to the Holy Spirit's power in changing lives for all eternity. They are tasting for themselves, the *feast of fire*.

The Harvest of Revival

As the days have turned into weeks, and the weeks into months, we have seen thousands of people from all over the world touched during the revival in a number of incredible ways. Who could have imagined that this great outpouring of the Holy Spirit would last six continuous months so far and continues even as I write this? God's mercy has been evident and manifest on everyone who has come to our church during this great revival. Over 10,000 conversions have been recorded so far as our nightly attendance averages anywhere from 2,300 to 4,200. Some 97,000 first time visitors have come through our doors as of this writing. Some nights capacity-plus crowds have packed the sanctuary, spilled out into the lobby and extended over into our chapel and cafeteria facilities. As a result, thousands have participated via closed circuit television, unable to get in the main building. On occasion people have had to park their cars a mile away. This revival, however, is about much more than numbers. It is about story after story of how God has touched individual lives in miraculous ways.

Drug addicts have been radically transformed, wealthy businessmen have been born anew, prostitutes and topless dancers have been changed and cleansed forever. The sick have been healed and the faint-hearted have been strengthened. We have even witnessed God opening the ears of two young boys who had been deaf.

Families have been brought together. Marriages have been saved. Teenagers have encountered the supernatural power of God Almighty for the first time in their lives, and children have come under the power of the Holy Spirit in unbelievable numbers, worshipping God with tears running down their faces, prophesying to their parents, and seeing visions of angels. We have been astounded especially at how the children have been touched by the Lord. It is both humbling and exciting to be a part of this mighty move of God.

82

Spontaneous Combustion

As we meet together for revival services, the format itself is not very different from any other church service: we have a praise and worship time, testimonies by either members or guests, a message from Evangelist Steve Hill and then a prayer time around the altar. What distinguishes these services, though, is the spontaneity and fresh work of God night after night. Every service is different. Every night the Lord moves on someone's heart to share his or her personal, powerful testimony. Every night we are visited by the Holy Spirit.

Sometimes Steve never gets to his message. We will experience such an attitude of worship and prayer that we will stay focused on God's presence for hours. People often cannot even sit up on their own strength during these worship times. And sometimes Steve's sermons will minister directly to certain individuals, leading us immediately into prayer times that often last until the early morning. Every night, one thing is certain, Steve opens the altar, first, for any sinner who wants to receive the gift of salvation and conversion.

I have never seen a man with as much passion for lost souls as Steve. He loves sinners with incredible depths, maybe because of his own sense of depravity before he came to Jesus. To listen to Steve feels like you are hearing a Finney or a Moody or a Whitfield because he has such a fervor for the lost. I have never seen a more effective altar call in my life.

After he leads the people through a salvation

prayer, the new converts are then counselled by trained leaders. We give them materials to help them in their new Christian walk and encourage them to become a part of a Bible-believing church. We record their individual names and addresses so we can follow up to encourage them and disciple them; and, of course, we encourage them to be baptized in water, making them aware that every Thursday and Friday night during the revival, we have a water baptism for new converts. These baptisms are incredible times of transformation and ministry by the Holy Spirit.

When the altar time for salvation concludes, Steve invites any first time visitors to receive prayer. Since we have been averaging hundreds of new guests a night, we pray for specific renewal or whatever need people request. It is during these prayer times that Steve and other Brownsville leaders walk throughout the sanctuary to pray for specific individuals. We have tried to give individual attention to every person who has come to the revival, believing God has brought no one here by accident. Steve will often feel led by the Spirit to seek out specific individuals or needs.

As God's manifest presence comes over these individuals, they respond in a variety of ways. It is similar, I believe, to what happens when a human body might hit an electronically charged power—the body often cannot withstand the brilliant force. So it is when a supernatural God manifests Himself on a natural human being: people are sometimes knocked over limp (or slain in the Spirit), some shake uncontrollably, others are rigid and tense. Sometimes people break out into tears or laughter, they dance or sing, they sit or stand. All are touched in accordance to their individual needs and the personal work of the Holy Spirit in their lives. This has been a beautiful part of this move of God.

Chapter Eight

Step Out of the Way

I prayed long and hard that revival would come to Brownsville. On a cool winter day as I prayed, I sensed the Holy Spirit speak, "John, if you *really* want revival, don't tell Me how to do it or when to do it. You'll have to step out of the way."

Yet I also remembered the instruction in 1 Corinthians 14:40, "Let all things be done decently and in order." And, of course, I reasoned, I had the proper definition of what was "decent and in order."

So imagine my perplexity when the Holy Spirit's expressions were different from what I expected. While I was preaching in the church I spotted one woman, her hands shaking repeatedly. I knew this woman. She was shy and quiet, and had only been born again two years. No one could have intentionally shaken one's hands for an hour the way she did; moreover she was not the kind of person to call attention to herself.

I remember seeing a middle-aged man fall on the floor and vibrate there for a full hour, sweat pouring off his face. I had known this man for thirteen years; he was a person of integrity, respected in his profession.

One woman in her fifties, from a staunch Baptist background, made repeated deep bows for more than two hours. This was a mature Christian woman, not given to emotion.

Another time a Baptist lady and her daughter came to a revival meeting. As they entered our church foyer on their first visit, the daughter was "slain in the Spirit," "resting in the Lord" on our plum colored carpet. The mother was so alarmed that she called for an ambulance to come and take her daughter to the hospital. The medics got the young lady on the cot, but as they jostled the cot in the ambulance, she came to her senses and mumbled, "Take me back. Take me back. There's nothing wrong with me. This is the Lord." They took her back, and she continued to "rest in the Lord," her mother later was amazed at the change God wrought in her daughter's life.

A Strange Spirit

But I have not always been open to letting God do things in His own way and time. I first had to discern what was of God and what was fleshly.

The year before revival came to Brownsville, an evangelist had called me. "There's a move of the Holy Spirit when I preach," he announced. I had already received reports from other churches where he held meetings. All reports seemed positive; people spoke of the Spirit's flow when he ministered. Hungry for revival, I had asked him to speak in a Sunday evening service.

I am a cautious man. Before we went to the

platform that night, I clearly stated, "Since I don't know you personally, I ask that when you are finished preaching, turn the service back to me. I can then lead the ministry time."

The evangelist soon started to preach on revival. His sermon was sound and Biblically based. Yet all was not well; a group of nearly 50 people had come with him, including the evangelist's team, and many who had sat under his ministry in other churches. Several sat on the front pew, with arms folded, staring at me while they punctuated the evangelist's sermons with shrieks of questionable laughter. Some stood up, only to fall to the floor. Their facial expressions and laughter troubled me.

Now I have seen and heard people "laughing in the Spirit" and "falling in the Spirit" all my life. When it is from God, these expressions of the Holy Spirit are sweet and orderly. But this was different. I quickly sensed a "strange" spirit in some of these people, manufacturing fleshly manifestations. I was hungry for genuine revival, not a carnal imitation.

During several points of his sermon, I considered stopping the evangelist from continuing. However, in honor of God's Word being preached, I kept silent.

Then the evangelist reached the end of his sermon. Instead of turning the service to me, he proclaimed, "Quick! If you want prayer, quickly come to the altar in front! Quick! I also need my catchers to come quick!" Before I could even get to the pulpit, he had already prayed for one woman who had come to the front, popping her on the head before she fell to the floor.

Time of Testing

I grabbed the microphone in hand and announced, "Ladies and gentlemen, this meeting is over. There's a strange spirit here tonight. I feel that the Holy Spirit has been grieved. This service is over."

Let me clearly say: I believed this evangelist to be sincere, preaching messages based on God's Word. I did not think that he should have continued with ministry time at the altar, especially after I asked him otherwise; but we can all get overly anxious and do things we would not do otherwise.

Most of the 50 who came to be with the evangelist were orderly. But not some; these were the handful I had to deal with.

After I stopped the service, three women and one man from that group of 50 stood in the church aisles and chanted, "Ichabod! Ichabod!" After chanting this Hebrew word meaning, "the glory is departed," they added, "God's going to get you. God's going to get you."

I was stunned by the response of this few, but knew I was right. "Ushers, come sweep the aisles," I instructed. My well-trained ushers herded this rebellious group outside on that mild May evening, but they continued to be vocal. "Leave the building immediately," I ordered.

Even during the service a few members from my congregation had become so upset that they had gone to the church foyer. The responses of this contingent frightened them. They knew I would act at the right time; but until then, they patiently waited in the foyer, often peeping through the doors.

Soon an usher rushed to me with a report: "The people we took outside are really angry. They're looking for rocks, bricks and landscaping ties, threatening to break church windows and doors. What do you want us to do, Pastor? Should we call the police?"

I paused and thought. "No," I replied. "God and His angels will protect us."

Several elders and deacons then came to me. Concerned for my physical safety, they formed a circle around me as I walked from the platform to the pastors' lounge. I felt their precaution unnecessary, but was deeply grateful for the care and concern of these godly men.

By the next day that incident was only a memory. The angry handful had left without doing any damage. But I was pensive. I learned my lesson: I needed to step out of the way, and allow God to bring revival in His way, through His people, and His timing.

What we experienced was invaluable: we saw the fleshly first, and didn't like it. Yet even then, we still hungered for revival.

From Glory to Glory

We soon discovered that when genuine revival comes, we must be prepared for new things. Scripture states, "But we all, with open face beholding as in a glass the glory of the Lord, are changed into the same image **from glory to glory**, even as by the Spirit of the Lord" (2 Corinthians 3:18).

Although God's character is changeless, He continues to bring change in our lives to conform us more fully to Christ's image. As we go "from glory to glory" in this life, there is change. **The next glory does not sound like, feel like, or look like the last glory.**

The Holy Spirit often does new and unexpected things; we have to "step out of the way" in our thinking and in our desire to maintain status quo. The same has been true throughout Scripture. When Noah built his ark, there had never before been a flood that covered the entire world, nor had there been a rainbow (Genesis 6:12-22). When Joshua and the Israelites conquered Jericho, the walls of a city had never before fallen that way, nor had God ever used a harlot to accomplish His purposes (Joshua 6). When Elisha helped the son of a prophet find his missing borrowed tool, a heavy metal axe head had never before floated in water (2 Kings 6:1-7). When Jesus was born, a virgin had never before conceived and given birth to a child (Isaiah 7:14; Matthew 1:18-25). When Jesus died and was resurrected, nobody before had ever died on a cross and come back to life (Matthew 27:35-28:10; Mark 15:33-16:14; Luke 23:44-24:51; John 19:28-20:29).

But as we go "from glory to glory," we don't always respond well to change, even when God is responsible. Remember Christ and the Gadarene demoniac? In Mark 5, we read of a man possessed by a legion of demons that left him so wild he was often bound with fetters and chains. Yet even chains could not hold him, for he broke them with demonic supernatural strength, and "neither could any man tame him" (Mark 5:4b). Day and night he roamed the mountains, often cutting himself with stones, running naked through the tombs.

Then Jesus met the demoniac. Jesus spoke the word, and those demons left that man (Mark 5:13). Jesus took what was abnormal, and made it normal.

Notice, though, the response of the people. When they saw the former demoniac "sitting and clothed, in his right mind, they were afraid" (Mark 5:15b). Instead of rejoicing that the man was tranquil and peaceful, they were afraid. Perhaps they had grown so used to the man being abnormal, that the normal man was frightening to them—almost as if they were more comfortable with him being demon-possessed than him being normal.

I learned that I must resist having the same

wrong reaction to the Holy Spirit's workings. As God takes us "from glory to glory," He will also take us out of our comfort zones. When new and different things happen, we must be careful that we rejoice, and enter into all God has for us. If not, we may never taste of the next "glory" God is bringing.

The Controversy of Pentecost

As God took the early church to the glory of Pentecost, controversy emerged. Onlookers accused those filled with the Spirit of being drunk (Acts 2:4-13). Their carnal minds could not understand these new manifestations of the Holy Spirit. A move and outbreak of the Holy Spirit has always caused misunderstanding.

After Jesus was baptized, when the Holy Spirit descended upon Him as a dove, He entered His public ministry. Throughout the following months, Jesus healed the sick, cast out demons, raised the dead, and fed the multitudes with loaves and fishes. Yet, although Jesus' words and works manifested the power and grace of the Holy Spirit, the religious crowd accused Him of having "a devil" (John 8:49).

Greed had turned God's house of prayer into a temple of merchandising. Jesus "cast out all them that sold and bought...overthrew the tables of the money changers, and the seats of them that sold doves" (Matthew 21:12). Then the blind and lame gathered around Jesus, and He healed them (Matthew 21:14). When the children saw this, they responded to the

Holy Spirit by crying; they shouted "Hosanna to the son of David!"

But instead of rejoicing, the chief priests and scribes were "sore displeased" (Matthew 21:15b) with Jesus. Jesus then pointed out that the praise manifested by the children fulfilled Scripture: "Have you never read, 'Out of the mouth of babes and nursing infants You have perfected praise?'" (Matthew 21:16; fulfillment of Psalm 8:2).

The religious people were raising a raucous about the children manifesting in the temple. Jesus rebuked them and defended the children's actions. The following verse states, "He left them" (Matthew 21:17).

When the Holy Spirit is present, people always manifest in different ways: such was true with Jesus, and such was true at Pentecost.

We Pentecostals have always been willing to be misunderstood because of speaking in tongues. But what about the other manifestations? Are we also willing to be misunderstood because of people falling to the floor, "slain in the Spirit", because some jerk, shake or tremble when the Holy Spirit touches them?

Are we going to be like David's wife Michal? She looked out a window and saw David leaping and dancing before the Lord, and "she despised him in her heart" (2 Samuel 6:16b). Instead of rejoicing with David as he manifested joy before the Lord, she rejected his actions as not befitting a king. Michal wanted a "home and gardens" religion, everything nice and proper; and Michal was childless until the day of her death (2 Samuel 6:23).

If you desire God to bring a genuine move of the Holy Spirit in your church, know this for a fact: controversy will come; and when it does, you have a choice. Are you going to respond with Jesus' anointing of continued obedience to the Father no matter what others say (even those you respect)? Or will you have a "Michal anointing," rejecting the Spirit's manifestations because they do not "befit" a believer, and remain barren in your spiritual growth?

It's time we believers be strong men and strong women of God, and realize that misunderstanding and controversy go with the territory. I do not want sterility in my soul, nor do I want the Dove to fly from my church.

The Witness of Church History

The annuals of revival in church history bear witness to God doing unexpected and controversial things. When revival came to Azusa Street, the following was written: "Proud, well-dressed preachers came in to 'investigate.' Soon their high looks were replaced with wonder, then conviction comes, and very often you will find them in a short time wallowing on the dirty floor, asking God to forgive them and make them as little children . . .

"Many churches have been praying for

Pentecost, and Pentecost has come. The question is now: Will they accept it? God has answered in a way they did not look for. He came in a humble way as of old, born in a manger." (1)

Read how revival affected some in Azusa Street. About one eight-year-old boy, it said the Holy Spirit "fell on him, and his hands began to shake and he sang in tongues." (2) It was further reported that "the meetings begin about ten o'clock in the morning and can hardly stop before ten or twelve at night, and sometimes two or three in the morning, because so many are seeking, and some are slain under the power of God." (3)

One quote caught my attention: "While some in the rear are opposing and arguing, others are at the altar falling down under the power of God, and feasting on the good things of God. These two spirits are always manifest, but no opposition can kill, no power in earth or hell can stop God's work, while He has consecrated instruments through which to work." (4)

The Holy Spirit's expressions, or manifestations, were not limited to the Azusa Street revival. "At a meeting recently held in a cottage near the church, one sister was baptized with the Holy Ghost on the front porch. She lay under the power of God for something like two hours, praising God and speaking in an unknown language." (5)

Daniel Williams recorded instances of phenomena in the Welsh Revival of 1904: "The manifestation of the power was beyond human management. Men and women were mowed down by the axe of God like a forest...The weeping for mercy, the holy laughter, ecstasy of joy, the fire descending, burning its way to the hearts of men and women with sanctity and glory, were manifestations still cherished and longed for in greater power. Many were heard speaking in tongues and prophesying. So great was the visitation in Penygroes and the districts that nights were spent in churches." (6)

In his autobiography, James Finley writes of the Cane Ridge Revival of 1801: "A great revival broke out in the state of Kentucky. It was attended with such peculiar circumstances as to produce great alarm all over the country. It was reported that hundreds who attended the meetings were suddenly struck down, and would lie for hours and, sometimes, for days, in a state of insensibility; and that when they recovered and came out of that state, they would commence praising God for His pardoning mercy and redeeming love." (7)

Physical prostrations and contortions were quite common under the ministries of George Whitfield and John Wesley. John Wesley wrote in his journal how Whitfield's initial alarm at these powerful manifestations later modified: "I had an opportunity to talk with him (Whitfield) of those outward signs which had so often accompanied the inward work of God. His objections were chiefly founded on gross misrepresentations of matters of fact.

"But the next day he (Whitfield) had

opportunity of informing himself better: for no sooner had he begun (in the application of his sermon) to invite all sinners to believe in Christ, than four persons sunk down, close to him, almost in the same moment. One of them lay without either sense or motion; a second trembled exceedingly; the third had strong convulsions all over his body, but made no noise, unless by groans; the fourth, equally convulsed, called upon God, with strong cries and tears. From this time, I trust, we shall all suffer God to carry on His own work in the way that pleaseth Him." (8)

No Different at Brownsville

"Manifestations" are outward, visible signs of an inner working of the Holy Spirit; they can either be responses or reactions to the presence or work of the Holy Spirit. We quickly discovered that manifestations in the revival at Brownsville were similar to what the Holy Spirit did in past revivals. After the Holy Spirit touched me in new ways, and I personally experienced many manifestations, I was more hesitant to stop and hinder others from doing the same.

Yet no matter what the manifestation, we found it helpful to ask five questions to discern whether it was of God or not:

1. Is Jesus being lifted up?
2. Is this creating a greater hunger for God and His Word?
3. Is this leading people to love God and each other more?

4. Is this bringing truth and greater spiritual depth?
5. Is there any practical change taking place (sometimes this must be judged over a period of time)?

We trained our altar workers, ushers and monitors how to recognize a genuine manifestation of the Holy Spirit, as well as how to deal with those who were reacting in the flesh. And while 90-95 percent of what has occurred in the revival services is genuine, my ushers and altar workers have had to take some aside and deal rightly with them.

As revival continued, we found nine "categories" or ways that the Holy Spirit expresses Himself.

Falling on the floor In the revival people often fall on the floor. Termed "slain in the Spirit" by some, and "falling under the power" or "resting in the Lord" by others, one does not have to look long to see that something is happening inside those "horizontal before the Lord." Such was the response of people like Ezekial (Ezekial 1:28; 3:23), Daniel (Daniel 10:9), and John (Revelation 1:17). After the ark was brought into Solomon's temple, "the priests could not stand to minister by reason of the cloud: for the glory of the Lord had filled the house of God" (2 Chronicles 5:14), perhaps indicating that these priests had "fallen under the power" of God.

The Holy Spirit seems to do a wide variety of

things in a person's life during this time: a renewed understanding of God's holiness, an inward healing of emotions, anointing for ministry, a giving of direction for life, a refreshing of God's love, and, in limited cases, the giving of a vision from God.

Shaking, jerking or trembling When the Holy Spirit began to touch others, they would respond or react by shaking, jerking or trembling. A few would shake or jerk their entire bodies; others would shake or jerk hands, feet, or heads. Such seemed to be the response of the men around Daniel (Daniel 10:7), of Jeremiah (Jeremiah 23:9), and of Habakkuk (Habakkuk 3:16). The psalmist suggested that the people of God should "tremble" in His presence (Psalm 99:1; 114:7), as did God suggest when He spoke to Jeremiah (Jeremiah 5:22).

We later found that something deep had happened in the person trembling, shaking or jerking—a dramatic change in attitudes, a cleansing of sin or of sinful habits. In the Brownsville revival, a number of children began to shake, jerk or tremble when the Holy Spirit touched them. The negative reaction of religious adults has been interesting. It almost seemed these adults would be more comfortable watching young people shaking on a disco floor in a night club, than watching them shake under the power of God in church.

Groaning and travailing Romans 8:26 explains, "Likewise the Spirit also helpeth our infirmities: for we know not what we should pray for as we ought: but the Spirit Himself maketh intercession for us with *groanings* which cannot be uttered." Paul wrote the Galatians that he would "*travail* in birth again until Christ be formed in you" (Galatians 4:19).

When the Holy Spirit expresses Himself like this in a person, it can sound like the person is heaving and in great pain. In reality, this person is praying, and might even be brought into a ministry of intercession. Groaning and travailing is nothing new in Pentecostal circles; I have been hearing this in church services since I was a boy.

Deep bowing Both Ezra (Ezra 10:1) and David (Psalm 35:13-14) bowed deeply before the Lord, and both were intercessors for their people. Even today you can observe Jewish people at the Wailing Wall in Jerusalem doing this. This manifestation is done in connection with prayer and is often seen in intercessors.

Heavy weeping and crying Scripture records that both Nehemiah (Nehemiah 1:4) and Ezra (Ezra 10:1) cried or wept heavily. God warned a sin-filled Israel, "Turn ye even to Me with all your heart, and with fasting, and with *weeping*, and with *mourning*" (Joel 2:12). The psalmist declared, "They that sow in *tears* shall reap in joy. He that goeth forth and *weepeth*, bearing precious seed, shall doubtless come again with rejoicing, bringing his sheaves with him" (Psalm 126:5-6). Many times heavy weeping or crying can be part of the process of repentance, healing inner hurts, grieving, or even intercession.

Laughing A merry heart is "like medicine" (Proverbs 17:22a), and laughter is a viable response when God brings one freedom: "When the Lord brought back the captives to Zion, we were like men who dreamed. Our mouths were filled with *laughter*, and our tongues with songs of joy...The Lord has done great things for us, and we are filled with joy" (Psalm 126:1-3, NIV).

We Christians have grieved and been oppressed so long, we've lost the ability to laugh. Unfortunately, the abnormal has grown to seem normal, and some believers reject "laughing in the Spirit." But greater healing and wholeness comes through holy laughter. Many occasions I have seen people "laugh in the Spirit," bringing with it a needed restoration of joy and love in their lives.

Being still or solemn King David frequently wrote of "waiting on the Lord," of "resting" and being patient in God's presence, of how he "quieted" himself (Psalm 25:5; 27:14; 37:7a; 131:2). This manifestation is a choice one makes in response to His presence. As one is still and silent before the Lord in revival, there is often personal, intimate communion shared, with God giving words of comfort, refreshing or instruction.

Being "drunk" in the Spirit At Pentecost, onlookers mocked and accused believers of acting drunk: "These men are full of new wine" (Acts 2:13). Paul instructed the Ephesians, "Do not be drunk with wine, wherein is excess; but be filled with the Spirit" (Ephesians 5:18).

Often, as with the believers who spent time in prayer prior to Pentecost, this occurs after spending a lengthy time in the Lord's presence. You sense the Holy Spirit so strongly that normal activity is difficult to perform. This also involves an inner work that God is completing, a 'breakthrough' that He has wrought. For me, the many times during this revival that I have been "drunk" in the Spirit, I have been unable to move.

Having visions and dreams These often take place while a person is "resting in the Lord." It can be similar to a trance, such as was Peter's vision (Acts 10:9-17). After all, Joel did prophesy that "old men shall dream dreams, and young men shall see *visions*" (Joel 2:28b).

When the Spirit is present in outpouring, visions and dreams are commonly reported among believers of all denominations. Even my own conservative sons, 19 year-old John Michael and 25 year-old Scott, have received several visions during the Brownsville revival. I know my own sons; they wouldn't fake it for anyone. And what God fulfilled at Pentecost is still true today.

Section Four

The Fire Spreads

*"Then I said, I will not make mention of him, nor speak any more in his name. But his word was in mine heart as a **burning fire** shut up in my bones, and I was weary with forbearing, and I could not stay." Jeremiah 20:9*

*"My heart was hot within me, while I was musing the **fire burned**: then spake I with my tongue." Psalm 39:3*

Chapter Nine

Let the River Flow

A few weeks prior to Brownsville's Father's Day outpouring and subsequent *feast of fire*, God led me to preach a series of messages that, in retrospect, I feel helped to prepare a Biblical foundation for what the Spirit was about to do. Because I understood why people sometimes perceive moves of God as emotional banterings with little Biblical basis, I wanted to make certain we stayed in God's Word. It is always both wise and safe to measure any spiritual outpouring against the Word of God. That is why I felt it was crucial to examine the Scriptures in a corporate setting in hopes of understanding more of God's work.

One Sunday morning, I spoke to our congregation specifically on the need for drinking from the river of God. I sensed that many in our church felt spiritually dry. They were thirsty for refreshment from the *Living Water*, thus I shared with them from Mark 5:1-15, the story of *The Demoniac of Gadarene*. Remember Legion?

"What is your name," Jesus had asked. "Legion," was the reply, "for we are many."

When the *spokes-demon* besought Jesus not to send them out of the country, remember that the Master exorcised them into a massive herd of swine that had been feeding on a nearby mountain. Consequently, the herd ran violently down a steep place into the sea where they all drowned. The people that fed the swine fled and told everyone what had happened. Soon a huge crowd came to see what was going on for themselves.

What do we gain from this passage? That the devil, or that demons hate water? In Matthew 12:43, the Bible says that an unclean spirit or demons roam about and traffic in dry places. They move where there is no water. They don't move in the desert just for the sand. They move anywhere there is no water.

I've wondered, "Well, Lord, why didn't you send them into the darkness? Why did you send these demons into the swine? Why did you give them permission to go into almost 2,000 hogs?" They asked that Jesus would grant them leave to go into those swine, but why did He give them permission?

When they entered the swine, something unexpected happened. The Bible tells us that the entire herd ran into the water and when they did, they drowned. As a result, the spirits could not stay. Demons hate the water.

Dry Bones

As a pastor, I know how God's people have been going through devilish situations, struggling with their families, their finances, in their marriages, their prayer and devotion time, and on their jobs. God's people have been suffering in many ways. They have been passing over dry places and what I want to point out is that demons thrive in dry places. How many of us have said, "I am so dry; I wish God would just send revival." Yes, the devil traffics in that same spiritual dryness.

There are many things which cause a person to become dry, but rather than waste our time on the negative I want us to concentrate on the positive. It's time we pressed on to victory! You see friend, I have good news. Change is coming! I believe a *move of God* is coming. In John 7:38 and 39, Jesus said, *"He that believeth on me, as the scripture hath said, 'out of his belly shall flow rivers of living water.' (But this spake he of the Spirit, which they that believe on him should receive.)"*

The Holy Spirit is that living water and the demons cannot stand it. If anyone is feeling harassed, or buffeted, it is because the *rivers of living water* are not flowing. The Bible refers to salvation as a well and we can live off a well. We can be thirsty and dry and let down our buckets into a well of water, pull it back up, drink and be refreshed.

Jesus said not only would there be a well but, *"out of his belly shall flow rivers of living water."* Not a trickle, but a river would flow, and if we have a river of the Holy Ghost flowing out of us, surely demons cannot traffic in our lives.

In the Bible, water is one of the symbols of the Holy Spirit. He springs up like a well, flows like a river, and falls like the latter rain. Demons are repulsed by the water of the Holy Spirit so they flee whenever the water comes. They thrive in dry places;

but where the water flows powerfully and freely, demonic forces have to flee!

Lake of Life

God said He sees the thirstiness of His people. He says He is going to open up rivers of His Spirit, not just normal rivers, but rivers of His Spirit to all who cry out to Him. He says that the wilderness will become like a lake of life.

Isaiah 35:7 says, *"And the parched ground shall become a pool, and the thirsty land springs of water; in the habitation of dragons, where each lay, shall be grass with reeds and rushes."* This passage proclaims the promise that when the needy and the thirsty cry unto Him, God will open up pools of water. He will then deal with the dragons and He will overcome.

In Isaiah 44:3,4, and Isaiah 35:1, God promises to refresh His people, to pour out His living water and to strengthen His church. We must say like Isaiah, "let the River come." We must let the Holy Spirit work in whatever way He wants to, for His glory, for His revival. Let sinners come to Him, let believers drink of Him.

I believe God is moving in a revival around the world. Some of us may clam up, or shut off the cisterns and flow of water, but I'm going to let the river flow. Thank God, it is time to let the river flow freely.

Chapter Ten

Warning Signs on the River

Revival is here. The *feast of fire* has begun. The River is flowing; but just because it flows in all its glory, winning the lost and reviving the church, the battle has not stopped. It never will subside in this life. I believe the enemy does not want revival to occur in America, and so pastors must guard against his attacks. We must learn to *pastor a revival* or else run the risk of wandering away from the River.

As a result of our participation in this fresh move of God's Spirit at Brownsville Assembly of God, I've realized that though the joy of revival is great, there are also numerous responsibilities that come with it. A flock needs a shepherd all the time, so a pastor cannot retreat from his duties just because God's Spirit has taken over. He needs to be aware of what it means to *pastor a revival.*

During the inital outpouring of the Spirit there are certain things Christian leaders must be prepared to come up against immediately in order to protect the flock and insure the work of God. I call them the *"Devil's Five Deadly D's,"* because if they are not understood, confronted, and dealt with up front they can dry up the outpouring of the River of Life.

1. Doubt

The first "D" stands for doubt. Suspicion, doubt and skepticism are all inevitable responses any time the Holy Spirit moves in a congregation in a new or unaccustomed way. In fact, in revival, people almost immediately will deal with doubt. This is not necessarily a bad thing. Though some might disagree, I believe doubt can provide a healthy opportunity to work through legitimate questions and concerns.

Doubt is a human trait that can be pastored for the simple reason that doubtful people do not know what to believe for sure. They might be uncertain, undecided or even suspicious about what is happening, but they are usually at least willing to listen and learn; however, I should point out that doubt is quite different from unbelief.

Unbelief is not the state of uncertainty; rather it is the state of believing nothing at all. For the pastor, unbelief is always much more difficult to work with. A sensitive shepherd can lead doubtful Christians and provide them with information from the Word and other Christian resources that will help them process their uncertainty. He can lead them into prayer and thus help to facilitate them in opening up their hearts to the confidence of God; but provide that same information and prayer time to an unbeliever, and no change will occur at all.

Unbelief paralyzes a person, keeping that individual stuck in inactivity. He chooses not to believe. A believer, however doubtful he may be, chooses eventually to believe the information presented to him. The unbeliever, on the other hand, will give up. Let me offer an example from the ministry of Jesus for your consideration.

There were several times in His ministry when Jesus could do no miracles because of the people's unbelief. Jesus knew, nonetheless, how to deal with those who doubted, like Thomas. Jesus actually helped Thomas and ministered to him to help him believe. He knew Thomas had some faith even though he felt doubtful. If Thomas had been in unbelief, Jesus would not have manifested Himself in the ways He did.

In the same way, Israel could not enter into the promised land because of their unbelief. They certainly had all the signs and information presented to them to believe; they simply chose not to. There will naturally always be doubters in any revival, but we must not let doubt turn into unbelief. Now let us turn to the second "D".

2. Distractions

When the Holy Spirit begins to fall on a church in a mighty way, there will be *two kinds of distractions*. First of all, there will be people who yield to bad distractions, such as watching an individual in a meeting who is drawing attention to himself or simply mimicking manifestations of the Spirit. They may even see someone who is in the flesh and as they do they may miss the 400 other people being moved upon by the Holy Spirit. The devil specializes in distractions, even in our closets of prayer; but in revival, it is as if the Holy Spirit is beaming down from the grand central station, and just as we are tuning into Him, the enemy changes channels to distract us.

The other type of distraction might be those normal, natural things which happen in our daily living. For instance, when we really love revival and want to be enjoying the presence of the Lord, satan will allow distractions in our homes or businesses that are legitimate, but they take our time and emphasis away from revival.

When Jesus healed on the Sabbath, the Pharisees could not enjoy the healing (or the supernatural manifestation) because it violated their code of strict conformity to religious law. They allowed their legalism to keep them from witnessing the work of God.

3. Disappointment

The third *Deadly "D"* is disappointment. When we are excited and exhilarated by what the Lord is doing both in our personal and corporate lives, we want everyone to get in on it. We want others to enjoy what we are enjoying. That's why we begin to realize a feeling of great disappointment when others reject what we are experiencing. When our children, spouse, family or fellow church members do not dive in as quickly to the River of Life, we can easily become disappointed. Worse yet, if they remove themselves entirely from the revival, it disappoints us and takes the wind out of our sails.

It also can be that things will begin to happen in our families, church or businesses that may not have anything to do with revival but they let us down. They bring disappointment. We then find it difficult to get back into the spirit of revival.

I have found some do not get back into the River of revival after they have been disappointed. I know many people who enjoy revival, but when they suddenly are an object of satanic attack or go through a fiery trial, they become disappointed and even disillusioned. They question, "God, how could you let that happen?"

Not long after revival hit Pensacola, two other powerful forces hit us. Hurricanes *Erin* and *Opal* struck us within weeks of each other not even a month after the revival had begun. Consequently, it distracted many people as they were forced to stay away from the revival services to repair their homes. Many of those same people struggled with getting back into the revival because they were so disappointed from the natural disaster they had just experienced.

Unfortunately, many Christians get disappointed that life goes on after revival; they just want to stay in the presence of the Lord feeling blessed, refreshed and empowered. What we need to recognize is that these times of refreshing come to help prepare us for the natural things of life, not keep us from them.

4. Discouragement

It is always a dangerous thing when people choose to wallow in disappointment. It can lead to discouragement. Discouragement leaves people depressed, cast down and suffering from a bad case of the blues. Even David prayed in Psalm 42:11, *"O soul why are you cast down?"* Discouragement will come to all who seek the Lord. Even Elijah, in the process of his greatest victory, was tormented with great discouragement.

I know very few people who are even-tempered. Most of us spend our time in either really high places or really low places. Let's face it, we go through emotional ups and downs and there's nothing wrong with that. We simply need to guard against staying in the lows. We must brace ourselves, especially in revival, for revival does not always bring joyous, enthusiastic changes. Though I have watched several powerful manifestations of God and witnessed one miracle after another, I also have seen myself and others grow discouraged in the process.

Discouragement is a trap and if we stay in disappointment long enough, it will lead us into a melancholy state and either make us discouraged or depressed. It takes a process to get us into discouragement, and it often takes a process to get out of it. We must not allow discouragement to rob us of all that God has for us.

5. Defamation

Finally, pastoring a revival is sure to bring on defamation. Numerous times I had to ask myself if I were willing to make myself of no reputation as a pastor. I knew people were bound to talk, mock and accuse as a result of the revival. Was I willing to take such assaults on my reputation? Could I live with the fact that other Christians were questioning my spiritual integrity and leadership?

A pastor and/or church leaders have to be on guard with this, especially if they are reputation lovers. If they want people to say nice things about them and brag about them, they need to be prepared for the times their character will be called into question; otherwise, it will be the knockout punch that takes them down. Many pastors can deal with disappointment, distractions, even discouragement; but they cannot stand to look bad in the eyes of others.

There have been some people during the Brownsville revival who have told me that they love what is happening at our church. They love the moving of the Holy Spirit and the manifestations. "But I do have a reputation to maintain," they tell me. "What will our friends say if they hear my daughter is shaking uncontrollably or my wife is dancing in the aisles?".

Every pastor wants to be respected in his community, revered for his integrity and esteemed for his faithfulness, but if revival falls, controversy will almost always follow, and one's reputation will be at stake. People will say, "Look, there's the pastor who lets crazy things happen at his church," or "That's the pastor from that weird church." So pastors who are thirsty for a move of God must also be prepared for the controversy and criticism that is certain to follow.

It seems like everything that we receive from God that is valuable and life-changing will require that we place it right back on His altar and one of those sacrifices may well be our own reputation.

Revival is indeed a marvelous wonder to experience. It draws us into God's presence and reveals to us more of Himself, but it does not come without a price. We must recognize that the devil will throw five deadly arrows our way in the midst of any mighty move of God, arrows that could kill or extinguish His move. We must pastor that *doubt*, guard against *distractions*, not yield to *disappointment* and *discouragement*, and be willing to suffer *defamation* just as Christ made Himself of no reputation. Thank God, we serve a God who is in the business of bringing life back from the dead. He is the Resurrection, and the River of Life.

Chapter Eleven

The Fire Is Burning — Now What?

Revival brings an abundant feast of God's holy fire. Those who enter swim fully in a refreshing flow of blessing and glorious grace. The River rolls and God's people move with it, but difficulties also come in revival. Some of these difficulties are natural, some are supernatural.

Let me assure you: pastoring revival is wonderful, but it challenges even the most dedicated shepherd. Satan not only blinds the minds of unbelievers, but he especially tries to distort and destroy God's work in the hearts of sincere followers (2 Corinthians 4:4; John 8:44); therefore, Paul cautions us to "Put on the whole armour of God, that ye may be able to stand against the *wiles* of the devil," (Ephesians 6:11).

Wiles are tricks, devices, gimmicks. The implication here is that of an evil blueprint or a concerted plan orchestrated by Satan for the deception and downfall of God's people. His purpose is to "kill, steal and destroy" God's work, particularly the move of the Holy Spirit during revival; so what about his schemes? What are the enemy's strategies against God's people after revival has broken loose? What are his tricks, his devices, his gimmicks?

As we entered the fourth month of revival, these questions filled my thoughts. Growing more and more concerned, I started searching my Bible for answers. Scripture records several powerful moves of God; times when the Almighty Creator Himself brought tremendous breakthroughs for His children. The Bible also shows how the enemy fought back, tracing his specific *wiles*.

This chapter outlines eight *wiles* the enemy uses to try to defeat what God is doing, even in the midst of the Spirit's moving. When revival breaks forth in your church, may you guard against these battle plans and stand firm in victory.

After the Red Sea Exodus—Came the Golden Calf

While Moses enjoyed a dialogue with God on the mountain top, the people of God were in the throes of deception on the plains below (Exodus 32:1-8). Their leader seemed long overdue; everyone's patience was running thin. Restlessness set in and then, remember how the spirit of deception finally took over? Even Aaron was convinced and without so much as a single protest the second highest spiritual leader in the land crafted a golden calf for the nation to worship. How quickly well-intentioned people became deceived.

Church, let me caution you. Get outside the perimeter of the Word of God and you get outside the perimeter of the Blood. Once this happens, it's easy to be swayed by evil doctrines and evil men. It may look good, sound good, feel good and even seem good, but it may not be God. Be alert. Do not be deceived. The first thing that happens during a revival is that the devil will come with a strong spirit of deception. Anyone can be deceived. Aaron was!

After Bread in the Wilderness—Came Dathan and Abiram

In the camp of Israel, in the midst of revival, rebellion rose up (Numbers 16:8-17). If not dealt with, it would pollute the entire nation, thus God separated Dathan and Abiram along with their entire families and all their belongings and the earth swallowed them up and the ground covered over them.

God will not tolerate rebellion; but when we humble ourselves and are obedient, He extends to us mercy, compassion and love. Holy Spirit, abide with me. Keep me in submission to the Father's will and to Thy wisdom and leadership.

After David's Kingdom Was Established—Came Adultery

Another *wile* the devil is always going to exploit during revival is sexual promiscuity. In the midst of a great move of God when emotions and feelings are already running high, be careful. Keep your passions harnessed. Exercise self-control.

While the church at Corinth was enjoying great spiritual success, it was reported commonly that sexual impropriety had boldly grappled its way among some members. Paul's remedy was to take immediate, drastic measures; anything was necessary to insure the sanctity and purity of God's people. Follow the Scriptural admonition, *"But put ye on the Lord Jesus Christ, and make not provision for the flesh, to fulfill the lusts thereof"* (Romans 13:14).

After Elijah's Fire—Came the Attack of Jezebel

Elijah, one of the greatest prophets of the Old Testament, wrestled with an insidious spirit that is still around today: *the Jezebel Spirit.* It is nothing less than spiritual intimidation. One of the greatest *wiles* satan will use against you is discouragement, disheartenment, and disparagement. Your enemy will beat you up every chance he gets.

Elijah ran away after one of his greatest victories (1 Kings 19), so the Lord sent an angel to reverse his discouragement. Afterwards, the prophet went forty days on the strength God had provided; but at the same time, he went forty days deeper into the wilderness. Elijah would not admit his discouragement.

At last, the Lord sent an earthquake, wind, fire and a still small voice. Still, Elijah would not be comforted; consequently, God instructed him to anoint Elisha to take his place. In the end, burnout and discouragement neutralized a powerful prophet's ministry. The devil is strong but God's Spirit is stronger! We must be wise to satan's *wiles* lest we become ineffective. If we dare to trust God, He will bring us through in victory!

After Nehemiah Builds the Walls—Tobiah Gains Position

God called Nehemiah to rebuild Jerusalem's decimated walls. While the people worked, vicious men taunted them. Tobiah was a pawn in the devil's hands, sent to manhandle and roughhouse those who would do good. Eventually Tobiah worked his way past the walls and gained a position in the temple, but he was eventually ousted (Nehemiah 13:4-9).

Be on guard. During revival evil persons, manipulators, will come along to distract and confuse. This is when the spiritually mature saints will prove especially useful. This is when the wisdom gifts of the Spirit must operate with cautious deliberation and sensitivity. We cannot put on blinders and allow anything and everything to come in; we must try the spirits to see if they be of God. Jesus warned that, if possible, even the elect would be deceived.

After Gideon's Victory—Man's Ministry Is Worshipped

Another thing you have to watch out for during revival is man worship. When Gideon suddenly emerged out of seemingly nowhere to become a great military genius, human tendency was to promote him to prime minister! *"Then the men of Israel said unto Gideon, rule thou over us, both thou, and thy son, and thy son's son also: for thou hast delivered us from the hand of Midian" (Judges 8:22).*

One thing is for sure and never forget it, God only gives the victory. He uses persons who yield themselves to him but the glory is never man's, it is God's. The revival is not about a healer or a miracle worker or a saver. Revival is about *The Healer, The Miracle Worker, The Saviour!* Man only gets the anointing, God gets the glory.

After the Miracles of Elisha—Gehazi Covets Silver

Covetousness made Gehazi a leper. Naaman was cured as he obeyed the instruction of Elisha. In exchange he naturally wanted to bless the prophet financially, but Elisha refused. Gehazi, Elisha's servant coveted the rewards and claimed them for himself. He got what he wanted; but he also was cursed with leprosy (2 Kings 5:20-27).

Revival has many great rewards. Sometimes we are blessed materially simply because we are responding to God with exceptional faith and we have engaged the laws of the harvest in our lives for the first time. We must be careful, however, not to become distracted by blessings. We are to enjoy them and use them with God's guidance, but we must always keep everything in proper perspective. Guard against covetousness.

After Gedaliah's Passivity—Ismael Murdered the Saint

This strategy is the silent killer of the saints, just ask Gedaliah. Here was a godly man, a governor, who was mercilessly murdered because he didn't take seriously the counsel of others. He knew the stakes; he had been warned, but he chose passivity (Jeremiah 40:14).

It's easy in a revival to get comfortable and feel secure. We think because the Spirit is moving all around us that we are immune to attacks from our enemies; but nothing could be further from the truth. Peter warned, *"your adversary the devil, as a roaring lion, walketh about, seeking whom he may devour:" (1 Peter 5:8).* Stay active, stay alert, be vigilant. Listen to godly counsel and resist the pride of a know-it-all spirit.

Enjoy the abundant feast of God's holy fire. Revel in streams of living water, the rolling river of blessing; but as you do, watch out for the *wiles* of the devil. He has a vicious battle plan and he is prone to attack anywhere, anytime. Be on guard against *deception, rebellion, sexual promiscuity, attacks of spiritual discouragement, wicked human manipulation, the elevation of man above God, covetousness and the perils of passivity.* The enemy's tactics are deadly and destructive; but God has made you *"much more than conquerors through him that loved us" (Romans 8:39).*

124

Chapter Twelve

Conclusion—The Fire Spreads

The *feast of fire* at Brownsville Assembly of God has spiritually nourished and refreshed tens of thousands. Night after night, we have come to the table, expecting to eat of God's presence and drink of His living water. He has not disappointed us.

As of this writing, I have no idea how long the revival will continue. We had no idea it would start when it did, or even last as long as it has. Thus far, I only know that God has visited us. I continue to pray simply that God would pour out His Spirit on every person who enters our sanctuary so that, in turn, His fire of revival might spread throughout the land.

Although no revival happens because of any human effort, there are several principles God's people can use to create an atmosphere where the Holy Spirit is more likely to move in a mighty way. Those principles include persistent prayer, building a proper foundation, expecting God to move, yielding to His Spirit, learning to pastor the outpouring, and continuing to pray for the harvest.

Persistent Prayer

What I experienced as a young boy growing up in Georgia and what I return to consistently as an adult is prayer. We must learn what it means to pray.

125

Every single night for two years, I prayed as a teenager with those godly men at Riverview Assembly of God. For two and a half years, I have joined my congregation here at Brownsville Assembly of God every Sunday night just to pray. Both times there was no other agenda except to pray. Both times God visited us with His power and refreshing love, manifesting His presence in spectacular and unexpected ways.

I believe a commitment to prayer, both corporate and individual, is essential for any mighty move of God. Revivals in history confirm this, the Bible demands this, and our experience in Pensacola validates this.

If anyone wants to see an outpouring of the Holy Spirit, I believe He must be prepared to get on his knees consistently and stay there. While there, he must learn to listen to God's voice, intercede for sinners and saints alike, and offer up petitions of faith and thanksgiving. Our congregations must move away from the weekly "prayer" services where we do everything except pray. We must cry out to God, as Paul said, constantly, consistently, thankfully and fervently. No other measure is more important to ushering in and maintaining revival. Nothing must hinder our prayers.

A Firm Foundation

In addition, we also must learn what it means to build a firm foundation on the Scriptures and on godly wisdom. No one showed me this better than Brother Wetzel. He molded in me a foundation of God's Word that has been an anchor through all the years. It has been the rock on which my life and ministry has been built, a lamp unto my feet and living water for my soul. The Scriptures have taught me how God's Spirit has moved, and will move, upon His people in these last days. Brother Wetzel, however, was not the only one instrumental in laying my spiritual foundation.

My mother, my wife, my brother-in-law (Reverend Paul Wetzel), my family, friends, and every congregation I have ever had the privilege of pastoring helped me build a firm foundation from which to shape a ministry for the Lord and a house of prayer for revival. Such a foundation constantly reminds us of the supernatural things of God; when we have tasted of His goodness, everything else is less than the best. We long for His presence. We thirst for His Spirit.

Expect God to Hear

From such a foundation, we learn to come to God expecting He will hear our heart's desires and prayers. As our congregation in Pensacola began talking more and more about needing a mighty move of God, as we prayed for revival to come, as I, Brother Dick Reuben, and Evangelist Steve Hill preached on it, and as Lindell Cooley and our worship team sang about it, we became more and more "spiritually confident," firm in our identity as children of God, certain of His ability to blow across our land. Though I wavered in my own personal faith at times not really knowing if God would answer our prayers. I was so thirsty for God that I had to expect His living water. We expected the Holy Spirit to move among us because He had said that He would both in His Word and in His people.

When revival really did fall upon us, we began to expect more of His Holy Spirit's tender touch and powerful presence each night. Why? Because we had seen how God moved on Father's Day, we believed He did not change and would continue to move in the same powerful, spontaneous ways. Granted, we in the 1990s have not seen the Glory of God descend upon us much. When it does, we almost believe it is abnormal. People are generally more comfortable with religious traditions and programs than they are with supernatural visitations of God, so many have learned not to expect any "disruptions," but when we expect God to move in our lives, and He actually does, it is not always comfortable. Let me give an example.

Some Christians might be more comfortable watching the body of a man on drugs shaking from the addiction than they would be watching the same man get delivered and start shaking because of the Power of the Spirit. In Pensacola, the more people see God's glory, the more comfortable, or confident, they get with it. Children have begun to pray with more faith than they ever had. Families have come together after parents expected God to reconcile them, and new believers are praying for others to be healed because they have watched God do the same in their own lives. As James says, *"When he asks, he must believe and not doubt, because he who doubts is like a wave of the sea, blown and tossed by the wind. That man should not think he will receive anything from the Lord: he is a double-minded man, unstable in all he does," (James 1:6,7).*

Yield to His Spirit

Having a humble expectation and confidence of God's ability is best reflected when we learn to yield to His Spirit. Because revival is often spontaneous, it requires that we get out of the way, submit our programs and agendas to Him, and give free reign to the Holy Spirit. On Father's Day, we did not plan to have church last until 4:00 in the afternoon. We planned on hearing God's Word through Steve's message, hoping some people would come to a new faith in Christ, and then praying for a few others. After that, we were going to go eat lunch with our families. Instead, we celebrated God the Father in a way we never could have imagined.

Many times since, we have seen this "spontaneous combustion" occur during our revival services. People will suddenly fall out of their pews during a worship song; they will dance around the altar without ever planning a step; they will shake uncontrollably as the power of God's Spirit descends on them. No one plans these things; they simply expect God to move in their lives however He chooses. As a result, the manifestations of the Spirit of God come in a variety of ways, similar to the outpouring of the Spirit on the day of Pentecost in Acts chapter two. So yielding or submitting our spirits to God's

Spirit is imperative for revival. We must learn to pray as Jesus taught in the garden, *"Not my will, Lord, but yours be done."*

Learning to Pastor a Revival

Learning to yield to God's Spirit also requires that a pastor give up his own pride and purposes as a leader. Only God Almighty can receive glory and honor for any movement of His Spirit during such a great outpouring as a revival. Who could hope for anything else?

But I also know that many human frailties and spiritual battles will come against us as we learn to pastor a revival. I learned early on that if God were going to pour out His Spirit on our church, and if revival were going to spread throughout our land, I needed to learn not to get discouraged or distracted in the process. I also knew if my own doubts were inevitable, there would be doubts among my people and that would bring disappointment. I had to be willing to submit myself, *(see Philippians 2:7)*, for the sake of the Gospel and the sake of the Spirit's outpouring. This meant loving my flock unconditionally, praying for them unceasingly, protecting them untiringly and serving them unquestionably.

Continual Harvest Prayer

If pastoring a revival starts with prayer, it

certainly continues with prayer as well. We must pray that the Lord of the harvest will send out workers to disciple our new converts. We must pray for the continued movement of the Holy Spirit to *"work in us that which pleases Him,"* according to Hebrews 13:21. We must pray for good fruit from the harvest, fruit that will last as God's people learn to abide in Him.

If there is anything that revival must accomplish it must be prayer, so that we might know Christ better. We must pray with Paul, *"I keep asking that the God of our Lord Jesus Christ, the glorious Father, may give you the Spirit of wisdom and revelation so that you may know him better," (Ephesians 1:17).*

God Has Indeed Visited His People

Many years ago, God drew me to Himself and allowed me to taste of His grace and mercy. Though I grew up without the blessing of a godly earthly father, God chose to pour out His blessing to me on Father's Day in 1995. I will forever be grateful for the blessing of such revival, this marvelous feast of holy fire that has come to us at Brownsville Assembly of God in Pensacola, Florida, and has moved throughout the world.

If these pages of my testimony and the story of the Brownsville Assembly of God revival help spread the fire of God's Holy Spirit across our dry land, then praise be to the Giver of all good gifts. May we know without question that the God of the Universe has indeed visited His people.

Notes

Chapter 8:

(1) Corum, Fred T., and Rachel A. Harper Sizelove. <u>Like As Of Fire.</u> E. Myron Noble, Editor. Washington, D.C.: Middle Atlantic Regional Press. (This is a collection of newspapers, 1906-1908, of the Azusa Street world-wide revival, currently published by the General Council of the Assemblies of God. These quotes are taken from page 1.)

(2) Ibid, p.1.

(3) Ibid, p.1.

(4) Ibid, p.1.

(5) Ibid, p.3.

(6) Hill, Steve, compiled by. "Collection of Miscellaneous Manifestations," from <u>The Prophetical Ministry (or the Voice Gifts) in the Church.</u> 1931, pp. 98-99.

(7) Strickland, W.P., Editor. <u>Autobiography of Rev. James B. Finley.</u> Cincinnati: Cranston and Curtis, 1953, p. 165.

(8) Potts, James H. <u>Living Thoughts on John Wesley.</u> New York: Hunt and Eaton, 1891.

For more information or to order additional copies of *Feast of Fire The Father's Day Outpouring* contact:

Brownsville Assembly of God
3100 West DeSoto Street
Pensacola, Florida 32505
(904) 433-3078